THE COMPLETE BOOK OF RUG BRAIDING

Joy of Living

THE COMPLETE BOOK OF

RUG BRAIDING

by Helen Howard Feeley

ILLUSTRATED WITH PHOTOGRAPHS
AND LINE DRAWINGS

Coward-McCann, Inc., New York

CONTENTS

To all the pupils whom I have taught, and from whose ideas, efforts and mistakes I have learned so much.

INTRODUCTION—THE BRAIDED RUG
HAS COME OF AGE

For years, visitors who came to New England during the summer felt that every braided rug they saw was beautiful in its own right, and quantities of mediocre mats were bought and called by their purchasers "lovely," "quaint," "typically New England," while they recalled, nostalgically, their early childhood when perhaps they had visited at the home of a grandmother. Their first recollections were of the braided mats in the homey farmhouse kitchen, and the mats would bring back the smell of jelly or the piquant odor of piccalilli or chili sauce, the wood chopping in the back yard and the pungent smell of nearby pines.

Perhaps it is the present day rush and the crowded hours of living all over the country, which make us pause when we see these simply constructed rugs and take us back to the simple life of the early settlers. The trend today of moving out of the crowded cities into the country is continuing at a fast pace, but how different today is the life there in contrast to the primitive living in scattered villages and small towns of one hundred and fifty years ago.

At that time, ninety per cent of the population lived on farms, and derived practically all their living from it—their food, their houses and the furniture in them, the linen from the flax they raised and the wool from their sheep. These last two items clothed them. Sometimes they bought a little cotton from the general stores or from a traveling pedlar who sold everything in the way of dry goods or household wares.

There were endless chores for all the members of the family with not an idle moment, for idle hands were not to be thought of when the farm chores were over. The women always had their spinning and weaving and their sewing. The stolen moments for their rug making from precious left-over pieces of cloth must have provided needed rest and wonderful relaxation. What dreams must have gone into all the "pick-up work" of those times. The braided rugs were born of necessity and could be made with no extra cloth or tools than those on hand, for woolens, cottons, linens, and linsey-woolsey all went into the same rug. Something was needed on those cold bare floors to keep feet warm during the bitter winters, and how comfortable it must have been to have warm thick mats under foot in the big kitchens which served as living room, kitchen, dining room, laundry and often a bedroom. These farmhouse kitchens were really the heart of the home.

Besides the utility of the mats, what joy it must have been to create something bright and gay, to lend an air of graciousness to an otherwise drab room. That eternal instinct of the homemaker led those women a long way from the bare floors to the cornhusk mats and the gay, cheery, warm, braided rugs. They may have been crudely made, according to present day standards, but the fact that this simple art of making a rug has survived all these years shows that women still love and enjoy the simplicity of such a handcraft, plus the inner urge to create something of their own. The rugs may have been very primitive, but they were in keeping with the simple furnishings of the farmhouses and the simplicity of the lives of those who lived in them.

Working by candlelight was not difficult for braiding. Many blind people or those whose eyesight is failing, turn to rug braiding as one of the crafts which demand the least in the way of eye strain.

The braided rugs of today are so different from the early ones that sometimes you hear, "What has happened to braided rugs like those we used to see?" Beautifully designed and blended rugs are now being made all over the country, yet have not lost one whit of the charm of the older mats. The technique is primarily the same, but just as every craft has been improved upon, so too have our braided rugs.

Forty-five years ago, it was common in New England to jog along in our first automobiles at the unbelievable speed of twenty miles an hour and note how the woodpiles back of houses in the country were protected from the weather by old braided rugs. Made of old clothes, clumsy braids with lots of raw edges showing, those rugs could not long withstand the wear by heavy farm boots or the beatings of the spring and fall housecleanings.

Yes, the braided rug of today has had its face lifted along with the old dry sink, the dough tray, the worn pine and maple tables and chests, the Boston rockers and countless other things out of the past. Today they are part of our every day living, but in all our rooms, a joy to have around us, especially because of our own work of restoration and our love of the traditional.

Since the early 1900s and particularly since the depression of the '30s, New England has been promoting more interest in the old handcrafts, and through various Leagues of Arts and Crafts, classes have been formed for instruction. Often the uninitiated looked upon these crafts as fads, but now the work turned out has become fabulous. New Hampshire has been especially forward-looking along these lines, with many centers established for selling the products.

Led by Massachusetts, the state-sponsored courses in practical arts have gone ahead at a fast pace, with both men and women learning the fine points of handcrafts in these evening classes and today in New England, there are many private groups, classes under church organizations, clubs, Y.M.C.A. and other state or town or privately directed groups.

The re-created village of Old Sturbridge, Massachusetts, shows craftsmen at work as in the early Colonial days and draws thousands of visitors every summer. In the same state, Storrowton Village on the grounds of the Eastern States Exposition in West Springfield is another re-created village, where, as in Sturbridge, all the buildings are old, restored homes, barns, meeting houses and shops of the period of the late 18th and early 19th centuries. At Storrowton country dances are held on the Village Green, and in July, a free Hooking and Braiding Bee is open to anyone who cares to come. This all day session draws hundreds of craftsmen every summer.

Exhibitions throughout the year draw thousands particularly to the rug shows, and many craft centers, especially in New Hampshire, Connecticut and Massachusetts, are open throughout the year.

Radio and television have been used to promote the crafts, and during the winters of 1952 and 1953, the Massachusetts Department of Education sponsored a series of half-hour television demonstrations by various craftsmen. It was a happy experience for those of us who were asked to take part in the programs, and there were many pleasant contacts from that half-hour's talk. The program was known as the "How Show," and that is just what it was, showing step-by-step techniques in braiding a good rug, stenciling a tray and so on, whatever the craft chosen for that day's program.

One of the first questions which is brought out by the eager, would-be braider is whether or not we must use all new cloth. The answer is No. Naturally, we shall use no worn-out or moth-eaten materials, but there are quantities of excellent woolens discarded each year because they are outgrown, outmoded, disliked, or because there is no place to store them. Rummage sales are filled with coats, suits and garments which may simply be faded though they are still in excellent condition.

Canvass your friends and relatives when you decide to make a rug. You may become very enthusiastic and find enough discarded garments to make a couple of scatter rugs or to give you a good start on a room-sized rug. Don't worry about the faded colors. When you know how to dye, you can rejuvenate any tired tan or droopy beige or faded blue and turn them all into glamorous-looking woolens.

The fever for braiding is contagious and has been for years. Right now we are experiencing the most widespread epidemic which has ever swept the country. Rug hookers have been inspired to create new original designs and they have been improving their work for the past twenty years, as they used their scraps to make beautiful "drawn-in" rugs. It is for that kind of mat that we shall save all our small pieces when our braided rugs are finished, so that we, too, can make some artistic hooked mats.

Right now, however, we are in need of room-sized rugs for the thousands of new homes which are springing up all over the country. No wonder this age-old craft is being revived, for the price of woolen rugs is prohibitive to countless numbers of our young married folk.

Some people explain this contagion of rug braiding as a natural result of the antique collecting craze, which, while always present to some extent, has increased enormously in the past quarter of a century. Go to any country auction in the summer, and look, listen, and keep your tongue in your cheek if you don't want to be the next victim of this fever.

At first, everything you see looks like a pile of junk and you feel you wouldn't take anything home if they gave it to you. But then you notice how apparently intelligent men and women vie with each other for the old tinware, the chairs with their seats missing, the dirty, worn-out-looking hooked and braided rugs, the old glass and china. You hear the smug remarks of the woman on your left who has just paid $15 for an old blue glass pitcher. You prick up your ears and decide that YOU need some education in the value of antiques.

Yes, the summer auctions send countless numbers of men and women to classes in the old handcrafts, and not only those who have been bitten by the antique fever. Love of a hobby, especially if it is a creative one, spreads to neighbors, relatives or anyone with time on her hands and a creative urge within.

Yes, the braided rug has come of age, and has gradually found its way into every kind of home, from the lowly farmhouse to the most modern of our present day houses. There is a design to meet the needs of the most casual way of living or the most formal. This homespun craft has raised its standards to the field of art, and we now consider it among the most prized of our furnishings.

The stores are filled with reproductions of Colonial pine and maple and cherry furniture which call for braided rugs. You may not own a single antique, but nothing can complement your present day furniture and pattern of living like a well-planned braided rug made just for you and your family.

THE COMPLETE BOOK OF RUG BRAIDING

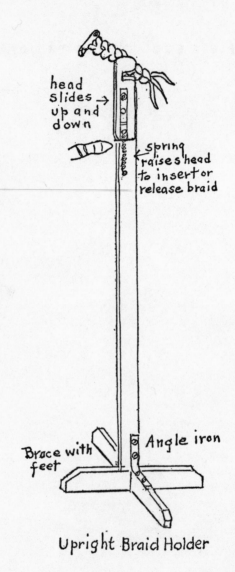

head
slides
up and
down →

spring
raises head
to insert or
release braid

Brace with
feet

Angle iron

Upright Braid Holder

1

OUT OF THE PAST—
A BRIEF HISTORY OF RUGS

The real origin of the braided rug as we know it today is shrouded in mystery, but let's look back through the years at the history of rugs in general.

In the Near East in the distant days of the earliest civilization, rushes were strewn on the dirt or clay floors to keep down the dust or to keep out the cold. As early as 6000 B.C., rush fabrics were used and these were plaited like basket work, which was one of man's most ancient arts. A tablet from Ur of the 3rd Dynasty mentions a reed mat in 2100 B.C. which measured approximately 10½ ft. by 18 ft.

These plaited mats became very popular and in mediaeval times in the Near East were dyed and commanded high prices. Even today in South India, excellent floor and sleeping mats are plaited of rush in beautiful colors. They are also plentiful in Mexico and South American countries.

Here in the United States, plaited mats made of cornhusks are still found outside kitchen doors of farmhouses. They have been made for several generations and are still made in Kentucky for the trade.

Sheep were domesticated in 7000 B.C. and tufts of wool began to appear in the rush mats, tied to the surface. In some sections of Asia, this type of rug still persists, and in South America among the Indian tribes, we find the same method used to ward off the cold of the high plateau regions.

The Babylonians wore cloth woven of woolen threads as early as 2600 B.C. The Assyrians were teaching the art of weaving in 2000 B.C. and by the 5th and 6th centuries B.C., we are told by Chinese documents that there was a flourishing industry of carpet-weaving in Persia and Central Asia.

To read about the fabulous rugs woven in those days for the great potentates is like a story from the Arabian Nights. The beautiful, intricate designs, the fine wools, silks, gold metal threads and even jewels which went into some of the court rugs make one ponder over the art as well as the arduous labor of years expended on o e rug alone.

The stories of those famous rugs is fascinating and well worth perusing. You will be amazed and delighted to find that some of the little patterns or designs which we use today in our braided rugs are to be found in the very ancient—as well as in the modern—Oriental rugs of the present time.

We read that the Romans were extremely proud of their woolen garments woven by the methods learned in their wanderings and conquests of Egypt and Asia Minor. In the Middle Ages, fine woven garments of wool, silk and cotton were brought back to Europe by the Crusaders, along with carpets and rugs woven by the Persians. Living among the nobles in Europe now began to assume great luxury, and we can't help but wonder if the serving women on those feudal estates did not beg fo the old, discarded clothing and save every last scrap to be tied into rush sleeping mats. The middle classes at that time wore clothing made of coarse homespun, something like our modern burlap.

Middle class women of those days braided their hair, but their mistresses had elaborate headdresses. For centuries, long hair kept its vogue, so the braiding of strands of cloth must certainly have been a natural craft in a time when strands of hair were confined by braids. And where is the boy or girl who has not picked up strands of straw in a field and idly plaited or braided them together?

Sheep were first brought into the United States by the Spaniards in 1540. They were raised in Virginia in 1608 and in New England some years later. As the population grew, more and more women in the colonies spun the wool from their own flocks of sheep and wove it into clothing for their families. Well-to-do folks had their cloth sent over from England. Cotton was not produced in any quantity in this country until after the Revolution. During the war and foɪ several years afterwards, dresses for women and shirts for men were made of linsey-woolsey, a combination of linen and wool.

When the modern woman thinks of the endless amount of work necessary to keep a family clothed a few generations ago—and large families were the order of the day—she pauses to admire the bits of handwork which have come down to us from that time and to marvel at the ingenuity and creative ability expressed by those homemakers of bygone years. The clothes, the homespun blankets, the mats for their floors may have been strictly utilitarian, which explains their scarcity, but the carefully stitched coverlets, the samplers and the crewel work rarely found today except in museums, are all expressions of their craving to beautify and adorn their homes.

Families living in New England became expert in spinning and weaving, for the winters were so rigorous that plenty of woolen clothing was necessary to withstand the bitter, cold weather.

During the Revolution, with supplies cut off from England, the need arose for "woolen manufactories" as they were called. These had become common in England since the new power machines had revolutionized the industry in 1750.

It was only natural that the first of these "manufactories" were established in New England where could be found not only fine spinners and weavers but exceptional water power as well. These first textile mills made clothing for our soldiers and caused a real expansion of the woolen industry. By 1810 there were twenty-four of these factories operating in New England and nearby sections of the country.

George Washington sent to Hartford, Connecticut, for the broadcloth, made to his order, for the suit he wore when he was made the first President of the United States. John Adams had his inaugural clothing made at the same place.

It was before the turn of the century that the art of braiding straw for women's bonnets from rye and oats was discovered by a Providence milliner, and before long, straw braiding had become big business in the neighboring Massachusetts towns of Wrentham, Franklin and Medfield.

At first the straw was parceled out to the village men and women, for everyone in the family braided in their spare moments. Horace Mann, as a boy in Franklin, Massachusetts, braided straw to help his widowed mother. At first, the braid was exchanged for staple articles at the stores. Later, "manufactories" had to be built to take care of this growing industry, and soon these "straw shops" as they were later called, were employing hundreds of young women "from harvest time to plantin' time."

Naturally, word spread to the relatives who had moved to Maine, and it was not long before the young women were flocking back to Massachusetts to work through the winter months in the villages which their parents had left after the war.

Having learned to braid and sew these strands together, is it too much to think that woolen rug-braiding followed closely in both Massachusetts and Maine? It was in this same part of New England —Rhode Island and southeastern Massachusetts—where the first successful woolen and later cotton mills were established. Soon, northeastern Massachusetts had its mills, along with New Hampshire, Maine and Connecticut. Vermont was to follow. New England had become the textile center of the country. No wonder the women there were adept at their rug-braiding.

They had long gathered berry juices or bought the cochineal dye for their red dyes and they used the butternuts, golden rod or onion skins for their yellows and browns, while the indigo which could be bought at the store yielded the heavenly blues which went into a young girl's best dress or the lining of a man's fine cloak.

Now, in the early 1800s, their cloth was already woven and dyed for them, giving the women extra time to use up those left-over pieces and carefully hoarded outgrown or discarded garments to braid into colorful mats to use over the bare, cold floors.

The woven rugs made on looms were made in strips and sewn together to make room-sized rugs, but some of the more ambitious braiders made theirs in squares and sewed them together to cover large areas, such as the 12-foot-square rug in the Dyckman House (1783-1785) in New York City. This rug is supposed to have been made in Peacedale, Rhode Island, outside the city of Providence.

Of woven rag rugs and braided rugs, the latter were considered the aristocrats of the floor coverings. Although carpet and rug weaving were introduced into this country about the same time as the textile factories, farm people did their own rug weaving and braiding for years. "Waste not, want not" was a well taught maxim, and to what better advantage could left-over cloth be put, than into rugs for the floors?

If one wonders why we do not find these braided mats of Colonial days, remember that they were made of any old pieces which came to hand regardless of the material. Woolen, linen, linsey-woolsey, cotton—all went into the same rug. It was a warm covering on their cold floors, and a craving for self expression. Little color came into their lives and the bits of bright rags put into their mats reflected their desire for a gayer life, a spark of cheer and warmth, to satisfy them through the long, arduous labor necessary for everyone who lived on a farm.

Most of the early mats were round like the crowns of the braided hats. When there were many rooms in a house, they were square and small, so the round rugs were well adapted to the shape of the rooms. The doors which we find in the early houses would have kicked up oval or square rugs, something which rarely bothers the women in modern homes today.

Occasionally, one found a rug made of straight strips, sewn together, with several braids placed around this center and squeezed in at the corners so that the rug was like a rectangle. Such a rug was made on Cape Cod around Marshfield, some eighty years ago.

Today, the craft of rug braiding is a national one, not confined to New England. There is a difference however in the styles of rugs made. The farther west one travels, fewer and fewer are the rugs which are butted, and larger and larger grow the braids. Speed seems to be the prevailing tendency of the times, and the continuous braid goes faster to the inexperienced.

Some women boast that they can make rugs—even room-sized ones —in six or eight weeks, but while the colors may be lovely, the wide braids look clumsy.

I have often been asked how long it took me to make different rugs.

"TRANQUILLITY" which is a continuous braid, square-cornered rug, 6 ft. 2 in. by 8 ft. 2 in., was made in six weeks, but I was six months working out my plan, garnering my materials and dyeing for certain effects, for I had to dye to match the colors in wallpaper and sofa.

"COUNTRY KITCHEN" which is just under 3 ft. by 5 ft. was made in ten days. I had all the material and none of it was dyed. I bought "a pig in a poke," for a friend who runs a mill told me he would have some headings for me on a certain day. I was gleeful as I left for the mill, but on my return, my spirits certainly needed a lift. I had not been allowed to choose my colors. The package was all ready for me and when I examined its contents, I found that out of around seventy-five pounds, I had eleven pounds of pretty blues, greens and odd colors. The rest were red, black and gray, colors which I certainly did not need. However, I worked out a rug which I felt might have been made in the old days when only those colors were to be had by the early braiders, and I put lots of design in it to show what we might do with three contrasting colors. It has been tremendously popular and has been copied in many states in many combinations of color. The rug is spiral in the center, then tapers off, and all the rest of the rows are butted.

One of the prettiest ones made in this same pattern used a soft chartreuse, a beige-and-brown mixture and a brown.

How long did it take me to make "COUNTRY KITCHEN"? All one night to think it out, and the next ten days to make it. The braids are less than ¾ inch wide. The material? Fleecy women's coating which I braided with the soft side out. It's lovely to walk on. When I see women putting this soft side on the inside, I think of all the domestic rugs made with the pile always having a lot of loose wool when the rugs are first laid on the floor. In time, wear of shoes and the carpet sweeper and the vacuum cleaner take it all up, but it is nice and soft for a while. Why don't we all leave that fuzz on the right side of the braid? When it is gone, then it will look like the wrong side anyway.

Many of the loveliest rugs made through the years are never seen except by their originators and their friends. One just hears of them, while the more mediocre examples are put on sale or into exhibitions. I have often begged women who have made unusual rugs to exhibit them but have usually met with refusals. "Something might happen" and they couldn't be replaced. It seems a pity that the rugs cannot be shared.

There is no question but that with more information about new techniques, the braided rugs of tomorrow will far surpass those of today and yesteryear. More is known about color harmony today than ever and there are many short cuts in technique. When we teachers say, "Look for color, design and workmanship," perhaps we *should* say, "Look for workmanship, color and design." Take time and do your work well. Let your rugs be the heirlooms of tomorrow.

2

STEPPING STONES—
MATERIALS AND EQUIPMENT

"Needles and pins, needles and pins,
  When a man marries, his trouble begins."

So goes the old rhyme, but my husband had an original version which he used to chant when he saw me sorting rags to make a new rug. It went like this:

"Scissors and rags, needles and pins,
  She's starting a rug, now we'll eat out of tins."

Times have changed a lot since I first started braiding forty years ago. So much really good food is pre-cooked and frozen that there are plenty of extra hours for handcrafts and hobbies.

One of the reasons which has endeared the craft of rug braiding to generations of women is that all the necessary equipment could be found right in the home. No frame was needed as was used for the rag carpets and for the drawn-in or hooked mats.

The rags came from the discarded and outgrown clothing of the family. It was unheard of to throw away anything which could be utilized. An old-fashioned flatiron, called a "sad iron," was used to hold the braid on the table to keep the tension taut, or it was braided without any help until long enough to step on or to wind around the top slat of a chairback. With feet braced on the bottom rung, this provided a good position for an even, tight braid to be made.

During Civil War days, the "sewing bird" appeared. Made of metal, the size of a little bird, it held a velvet pincushion on its back, a spring in its beak to hold sewing or braid, and a clamp on its feet which could be attached to a table.

We use the same equipment today with a few changes and additions which ease our work and speed up the time we spend in making our rugs. What used to be a winter's project can now be done in a few weeks. We make small braids like the best of those made by our great-grandmothers; we turn in all our raw edges; and we lace with a heavy thread which no longer cuts our hands or our cloth.

equipment

Our necessary equipment today includes essentially the same things as those listed above used one hundred years ago, with a few changes and additions:

medium-sized scissors
long, thin darning needles
heavy lacing thread
thimble
small pair of pointed pliers
clip-type clothespins
metal cones (braid-aids)
color guide
cutter

medium-sized safety pins
heavy-duty thread in assorted colors
lacer or blunted darning needles
measuring guide or ruler
braid holder to fasten on table or armchair, or one to stand in front of your chair.

Let's look over some of these new aids to braiders. The lacers, which are narrow and curved, work the fastest especially when the braids are tight. The blunted darning needles will sew or lace, no matter how small or how tight the braid may be. There are many kinds of lacing thread on the market. I like the 16 ply woven-cotton thread which comes in pound or half pound cones, and in black, brown or linen color. It has been on the market about four years but has become very popular. Made especially for the braiders, it will not cut the hands or the cloth the way linen and nylon do.

Our braid holders, though not as pretty as the sewing birds, are made of metal or of a combination of wood and metal, or all wood. We can fasten them to the edge of a table or an armchair, or we can use the upright model which stands on the floor and is just the correct height for us to use as we sit in our easy chairs. For those who go out visiting with a group and for whom no table is available, or for those who want to watch television as they braid, these standing braid holders are ideal. (Fig. 1)

The cutters are like those used by the hookers to slit their cloth, except that the ones for braiding will cut your material up to two inches wide. You can even buy a combination cutter which may be used for hooking and braiding just by changing the cutting blades. Torn strips have softer edges to turn in.

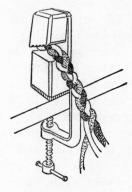

FIGURE 1

There are many commercial color guides to help you know something about colors which may be used together for harmonious blending or accents in your rug through the use of opposite or complementary colors. These are well worth having and studying.

The metal braid-aids are cone- or flat-shaped and have come into popular use during the past dozen years. Unfortunately some people seem to expect them to not only turn in the raw edges but to braid without any effort on their part at all. If they are used correctly, they can be of great assistance to those who are not too adept with their fingers, those who have weak wrists or arthritis in their arms, wrists or hands, or to any beginner learning this age-old craft of braiding. Instead of metal cones, the Redi-Braid Co. has developed plastic holders, which also hold a 15 ft. roll of cloth. This takes care of turning in the raw edges, and unwinding the rolls, without any tangling of strands. When used properly, these aids make a small, neat braid, for all the materials are of the same weight and quality and are cut 1½ inches wide.

If these braiders are put on the strips with the cloth the correct width or even a tiny bit wider so that it will not slide around, if the open folds are kept always to the right and are not allowed to swing over to the back, and if the braider will keep them just below her hands and will pull her braids tight instead of letting the folds fall where they will, the braid-aids can be of real value in easing the work and of speeding up the braiding. But don't expect gadgets to do everything for you.

Although I am one of those older braiders who learned to use thumbs and forefingers in turning in raw edges and in making a small braid firm and tight, I turn to these metal cones when I am making multiple-strand braids. It takes too long to turn in and stitch the edges of five or six strands with long basting threads as I used to do. Now I slip on the braid-aids, for I cannot manage a neat braid and turn in the edges of all those strands at the same time.

For those who make large braids from heavy overcoatings or blanket materials, it is far easier on the wrists to use these metal cones. There is one thing I must caution all to watch for, and that is the "tweaks"—or creases—on the wrong side of your braids. Those who lace on the wrong side of the rug will see these tweaks and correct them, but too often a worker will braid and lace on the right side of the rug, never turning it over to see how the other side looks. If the material is too thin or has been torn on the warp (lengthwise) instead of the pic (selvage to selvage) which has more "give" to it, there will undoubtedly be creases on the other side. If the braid-aids are not checked often to see how well the raw edges are being turned in, this process may not be done evenly on both sides. This also gives resultant tweaks because while there are only two thicknesses in the middle of your fold, there will be four on the outside of the strand. Open the strand often, whether you use braid-aids or not, to check this important point in good braiding.

When nearing the end of a strand, you must be careful to push up the braid-aids to allow yourself a length of cloth so as to attach a new strip. Then pull the aid down again, flattening the seam out with your fingers.

While I find both round and flat braid-aids are used by many women, I think the rounded ones are easier for the majority of braiders. However if your hand is quite large, you may like the flat ones. Some women like to keep the cones in their hands, with the open sides towards the right. They seem to think there is less danger of tweaks in this way. Some of these braid-aids are adjustable for various weights of materials.

But whatever you use and however, draw your strands tight as you go along to insure close small braids.

materials and preparation

When I first became interested in rug braiding, I went to a woolen manufacturer and asked for information about various kinds of materials. A few of the points which I learned from him have been of tremendous help in my classes. With samples, I have been able to show why some cloth will wear much better than others.

The hard-finished worsted woolens which you will find in men's good suits are made from long staples of wool and they have a finish which gives them a smooth look. These are expensive but wear beautifully. In rug braiding, they are apt to tweak because of this hard finish but they can be lined with a piece of soft wool to fill them out. I have rugs made of old suits which have seen hard service for twenty-five or more years and the cloth has no breaks in it.

Closely woven woolens will give more satisfaction than thinly woven cloth such as basketweaves which allow dirt to sift through. Many materials are beautiful to look at or wear as clothing, but remember you are going to walk on your rugs for years. Unless you put in sturdy cloth, they will be worn out in a few years.

Woolens with rayon threads are fine to use but the rayon will not wear as long as the all wool. Tweeds are pretty but be sure to buy the heavier ones. Fleecy materials are soft and wonderful to use. Be sure, by looking at the back, that you have selected only those with firm, closely woven threads. Use the heavier flannels, plaids and checks made for outdoor sportswear for men.

Some of the less expensive woolens are reused wool. They feel coarse, the staples are short, and they are used for boys' cheap clothes and inexpensive blankets.

Reprocessed wool materials should be avoided. They are made from waste and your long hours of work will soon show wear, for the short fibers will kick up. Jersey in a rug gave me the poorest-wearing rug I ever made. Avoid it. There is too much stretch to it. It is all right for a table mat. We also can use old silk or nylon stockings for these for they do not have the hard wear of a rug underfoot.

Army and navy uniforms which have been outgrown or are lying around unused are excellent materials for rugs. I can always count on pupils turning up with plenty of khaki, marine green and navy cloth, far superior to anything they could afford to buy today. The light-weight blankets too are being used to advantage.

If you are buying all your materials, try to choose those which weigh from 14 to 16 ounces to the yard. The more uniform the weight, the easier it will be to have a smooth-looking rug with the same width braids and no lining.

Woolens are woven from 54 to 60 inches wide, and your pieces will be better to work with if the fabric is torn from selvage to selvage. There is more suppleness in woolens torn in this way and there is not so much danger of tweaks or creases on the wrong side. When clothing is made, skirts and trousers are cut on the length of the material to avoid this stretching of the cloth which would result if cut on the width. Of course if you are using old materials, you would tear the long way of an old pair of trousers and use lining to prevent the resultant creases. The only way to avoid having to use these linings is to tear very wide and then crush in or roll in the outside edges to the middle of the strand.

Most woolens tear easily and for braids not over ¾ inch wide, I suggest that you use 1½ inch-wide strips. If the material is a little firmer and thicker, such as suede or doeskin or fleece-finished, use strips 1¼ inches wide.

When you make that first snip in your cloth with your shears, using your measuring guide (which you can make like Fig. 2 from a piece of cardboard), be sure that your shears do not cut just a thread wider or narrower than what you want. As you start to tear, check the width, for the shears often snip at an angle. If there are rayon threads, watch out that you do not pull out the threads if you tear too slowly. Best to tear very fast with cloth like this, or to cut all the strips by hand or with the cutting machine.

Our finest old braided rugs and the ones which have lasted the longest, were made of small braids, sometimes as narrow as ½ inch. If you are one of those who want very wide braids—and I hope there are not many of you—tear your strips into at least 2 inch-wide strips. Do not cut or tear all your materials at once. With three strips, start your braid. You may find that a strip may need to be just a tiny bit wider or narrower than what you thought. Better to rectify this matter now than when *all* the fabric has been torn.

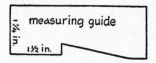

FIGURE 2

When you have definitely decided you want to make a braided rug for hard wear, the following suggestions will help you when you go to a remnant store or a mill-end shop and see those bales of beautiful colors just being unpacked: try not to be carried away by the various shades; be more discriminating about the materials; and if you can't find the colors you seek, buy the whites, beiges, grays (in plain colors or tweedy mixtures), the pale pinks if you are looking for rose or rust shades, and pale blues if you can't find the greens you need. These can be dyed later and you will have exactly the shades you need for blending colors.

It is not necessary to buy all the cloth you need at once, especially for a room-sized rug. It is expensive and you might change your mind about certain colors before the rug is completed. If you have a color chart, you are off to a good start, for you can better gauge the amount of each color which you will need.

If you buy narrow strips by the pound, allow 20% waste. For example, if you purchase ten pounds of materials, you will find you have two pounds of narrow strips or uneven edges left over. These can be kept to use as "fillers" or can be put aside to use if you make hooked rugs.

I have given this information about woolens because almost everyone wants to make a rug with a long life to it. But some will ask, "What else are little rugs made of?" and I answer, "Woolen or cotton, rayon or silk, velvet or cornhusks, or cloth made of milk." We can use any of these plus the endless synthetics appearing constantly on the market, but let's not try to put them all into the same rug. We must always consider the spot where we wish to use it.

We may want a silk mat or a velvet one to use under a table lamp; a rough cornhusk mat for the porch just outside the kitchen door; a washable one of denim or pretty cotton prints for the bathroom; chair-seats of old stockings dyed in various shades, or woolen ones flecked with metallic threads, or sturdy woolen ones for practical purposes for any room in the house.

The new synthetics have not been in use long enough for us to advocate their durability as materials for rugs. But as for their beauty and texture, no one will deny that they are lovely to look at, while the rayon and metal threads give a lively look and a rich sheen to what otherwise might be very ordinary fabrics.

If you are using old materials, you will have a little extra work in preparing them for braiding. Some teachers frown on anyone's bringing to class a lot of old woolens with which to braid a rug. I think this is a wonderful project. If the garments were good, they may be a lot better than the woolens you can afford to buy at today's prices, and that old maxim of "waste not, want not" is still as applicable as ever.

Countless numbers of old coats, bathrobes, suits and other wool clothing are discarded every year, not because they are worn out but because they are outgrown, outmoded, faded, or because of small tears or rips in conspicuous places.

One of the most satisfactory rugs ever made in any of my classes was a good-sized scatter rug which cost $1.65 including the thread and a package of dye.

When you use old materials, you must rip up all seams, remove buttons or other trimming, cut out all worn or moth-eaten places, wash well in warm, soapy water and rinse in clear, warm water. Hang in the fresh air if possible to help blow the wrinkles out and avoid pressing. Yes—there's more work in using old clothes, but there is a wonderful satisfaction in knowing that you will have a handsome rug made with strict economy.

3

TRENDS IN TECHNIQUES— OLD AND NEW

All craftsmen can improve their techniques by watching others work, by hearing of new ideas and absorbing them, by reading of different methods and through the exchange of ideas. No one person knows the "last word." Some people are ingenious and are forever seeking short cuts and improvements upon old ideas, while others are content with whatever comes their way so they can merely copy.

Progress can be made by trying out different schemes, whether it is endeavoring to make a specially shaped rug, joining the ends of each round, a process which we braiders call "butting," attaching the first two braids of an oval or rectangular rug, or working with any one of the various techniques which we must settle on when we make these rugs.

Each braider knows whether or not she wants three rugs in that long living-dining room of hers, or one large wall-to-wall square-cornered rug of three strands, or a multiple-strand floor covering which works up so fast. The latter were popular generations ago with the women who wanted something "different" and centuries ago they were made of rushes plaited to cover the entire floor. Today, some women feel they are the answer to a quickly made floor covering which is decidedly eye-catching and unusual.

However we make our rugs, let's have them substantial, blending harmoniously with their surroundings, artistic and practical, the results of good colo , design, materials and workmanship.

Are you a plaiter or a b aider? Many women do not know there is a differe ce. They have learned one way and they do not see any difference in the finished products until they are pointed out. In appearance, the most noticeable one is that, in a plaited rug, the open folds are al. in the center of the braid; while those of the braided strands are either all to the left or to the right and are hidden when the braids are laced together. The old cornhusk and rush mats were plaited and in Canada, northern New York and on the Cape in Massachusetts, one still finds many braiders making their rugs in this fashion.

The now obsolete English word "bredan" meant to move the hands back and forth quickly, and that is just what we do when we plait or braid.

In plaiting, one uses the wrist, elbow and shoulder to give an outward twist of the wrist as the strand is swung up and turned over to the other side, then laid down so that your forefinger is on top. The open fold is either toward the start of your braid or facing you as you work. There is much more motion to this method and the braids do not lend themselves easily to lacing without skipping every other loop on adjoining rows. This lacing leads to loose dirt pockets.

Hair has always been braided much as the gold and silver wire was braided centuries ago by the Egyptians when they made their jewelry. These mediums do not lend themselves to being raised up and turned over like the more pliable rushes which are braided when dampened, nor can short ends of hair be kept smooth with plaiting.

For those who prefer to braid, we simply pull the outside strands with a slight outward twist of the wrist over the middle strand. We work almost entirely at the sides. As we grasp each strand with thumbnails showing, we never lose sight of them. In plaiting, though we start with our thumbnails in sight, we turn them under and complete a loop with the nails of our index fingers on top. Try to braid and see which you are—a plaiter or a braider.

I used to plait until about a dozen years ago when I had bursitis and arthritis in my right arm and shoulder. I changed from plaiting flat ½ inch-wide braids to braiding the round braids ⅝ to ¾ inch wide, and in a few months my troubles disappeared.

The straw workers in southeastern Massachusetts made the round braids and the craft was passed on to the relatives in Maine, and in these states little of the flat plaiting is to be found in comparison to the round braids. At an exhibition of state-made crafts held in Camden, Maine, about fifteen years ago, there were many braided rugs on display but very few plaited ones.

Use of the braid-aids is helping many women to braid instead of plait. This makes lacing so much easier than the slow, painstaking sewing. No longer does one hear the old expression "I'm pleatin' a rug" which was common in Vermont and New Hampshire years ago. I have yet to find a single braider who has gone back to the plaiting of a rug once she has learned how to braid.

Practically everyone now tucks the raw edges out of sight between the folds whether it is done with the thumb and forefinger as I was taught years ago by my mother, or whether it is done for you automatically by the braid-aids. Some still keep their open folds on the back or wherever they may fall. They never turn over the braid to the wrong side to check this point or to see if the braid is smooth, yet these may be the very rug makers who are using thin or hard-finished materials which tweak or crease and which should be lined. A filler is simple to use if you are not using braid-aids and some women use the fillers along with the adjustable braid-aids. Use a soft, narrow, ½ or ¼ inch-wide strip of wool, matching the color as near as possible, and put it right in the middle of your strand. It will fill out the braid.

Watch your raw edges constantly to make sure that they are being tucked ALL the way back to the center of the strand. You want four thicknesses of cloth throughout the strand. This lack of four thicknesses will make your braids uneven and full of creases on the wrong side. They will also give you an uneven surface.

start of the braid

Have three strips of unequal length to avoid having three seams coming at the same spot—this would make a bulky place in the braid. If you have torn your cloth from selvage to selvage, the chances are that the materials will be of different lengths if you have used three different weights. There is more give to the tweeds which may run from 54-60 inches wide. If you find that they are all the same length when you reach the ends, cut them in different lengths before joining on the new pieces.

If you are going to use braid-aids, slip them on at once before you enclose the start of your braid. You can make either a "sore thumb" or T start which is good for a round rug, or the "enclosed ends" which I like for ovals, rectangular rugs and for all butted ends.

"sore thumb" or T start

To make the T start, cut the ends of two strips on a bias and stitch together. Press the seam flat and turn the raw edges to the middle. Take the third strip and turn in to the middle. Now turn in once more to the middle. Lay this Strip 3 inside your straight double strip forming a T. Stitch in place. Keep the open fold to the right, or if you prefer to braid with your open folds on the left, turn Strand 3 that way. If you have never braided before, try to braid with these open folds on your right. There will be fewer pitfalls for you, especially if you use the braid-aids. (Fig. 3)

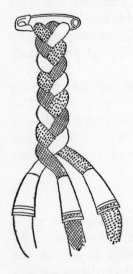

FIGURE 3

Start either with the strand at your right or at your left—it really doesn't matter—whatever seems to be the most natural for you. Draw over the center and then, holding down with the thumbs, draw the other outside one over, forming a sort of hood. This opening must be kept on the same side as the first strand. The middle strand is the

last to be drawn around. Once this has been accomplished, put a
medium-sized safety pin in the top from right to left so that the
open side—or nose—points to the left. This will be a guide for you
in many ways, so do not forget it. Once you have made the first three
turns, you will find that in braiding you take the strand at the bottom
and bring it around the side over the one on the top, always remembering to keep those thumbnails in sight, and swinging outward and
inward quickly with your wrists for a firm, tight braid.

enclosed ends

If you do the "enclosed ends" which is the method I use the most,
you will turn each strip to the wrong side (put on the braid-aids first
if you plan to use them) and stitch by hand or machine across the
edge and down the side about an inch. (Fig. 4) Use backstitch or

FIGURE 4

overcast. If you backstitch, it will be softer than the machine stitch
or overcasting. Be sure to use matching thread and sew close to the
edge. With your pliers or scissors or eyebrow tweezers, turn to the
right side, making sure that the enclosed end is straight across. Push
in the open fold side to the center. Do this to all three strands and
put onto a safety pin with the open folds on the right or left as you
wish, preferably on the right if you have no choice. Put the pin
right through the seam and through the middle of the cloth. (Fig. 5)

Number these strands in your mind from left to right as 1, 2, 3.
Grasp 3 with thumb and forefinger of right hand, tucking raw edges
inside the fold with your thumb. With forefinger, fold in open side
of 2 and swing 3 over 2. With right thumb, hold 3 over 2 as you

tuck in raw edges of 1 with the thumb on your left hand. Draw over 3. Using your thumbs and forefingers, continue in this way, taking the strand from the bottom and swinging it over the top strip.

If it seems more natural to start with the strip at your left, do so by all means. I do both equally well. I change from one to the other according to the way my pupils work. Some find it very awkward to braid with open folds on the right; some just can't seem to braid with them on the left. But if you use the braid-aids, do practice using the open folds on your right.

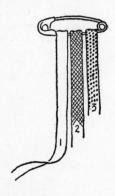

FIGURE 5

Braiding a straight braid should be practiced until you can make a neat, small, uniform braid. Do this before you start a rug or even a chair seat and you will be well repaid for the few extra minutes it takes to become accustomed to handling the three strands and to tucking the raw edges out of sight with your thumbs and forefingers if you do it by hand, or working with the braid-aids if you use them. (Fig. 3)

There are all sorts of cumbersome holders for woolens on the market, but two paper bags on the floor beside you for holding your balls of material are better than any of the fancy and expensive things I've seen. A third roll of material can be kept in your lap. If you have your material all rolled up and the ends sewn together on a bias and trimmed before you start to braid, it saves time. Press the seams out flat with your fingers and keep rolled on the wrong side.

These seams are almost always hidden in the folds, and if one comes in a bad place—such as the top of a fold—cut off a small length and put the seam where it will not show.

These bias joinings can all be done on the sewing machine if you wish. Save time by doing several while you are about it. Do not break the thread. Just keep adding strips. (Fig. 6) When you have added all you want, you can snip the threads and trim the bias seams, saving the little triangular pieces to make your color guide.

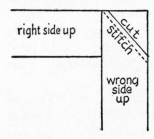

FIGURE 6

The roll in your lap will stay in position if you run a very narrow strip of cloth or a string or your heavy lacing thread through the hole in the center and tie gently. As you use the material, it will unwind for you but not come undone. Many women like to add new strips as they go along, sewing them by hand. Be sure to sew firmly, so there will be no possibility of the seam coming apart.

Years ago when we sewed our rugs instead of lacing the braids together, we had to use strong needles, and working on the wrong side, we would sew through the folds with close invisible stitches in order to have the rugs perfectly reversible. This was hard work on the fingers and hands, but made much nicer looking rugs than those sewn with a faster over and over stitch. Threads against a hard surface like a wooden floor are bound to wear out, but tucked out of sight between folds, they have far less wear on them.

continuous or spiral rugs

Many rug braiders—and this is especially true of the men—make a rug the desired size and taper it off to end it. In New England the butted rugs are common, but the farther west one goes the larger grow the braids. Many of us have made our rugs butted from the first two rows, but it is now a common practice to make the center in a continuous braid, then taper it off and butt the rest of it. Sometimes a rug is continuous until the maker wants a solid band. Then she tapers off and butts the rest of her rug. Even if large rugs are made with many tweeds pulling the solid colors together, the last few rows will look better and the rug will be more symmetrical if they are butted. This certainly gives a finished, tailored look to the rug.

It is a little more work to turn the rug over and lace on the wrong side but well worth that bit of extra effort. The side which is laced is always flatter and does not have the depth of color which the other side shows.

For years I have been trying to put that across to those who feel it is too much extra effort to lace on the wrong side. When a rug of mine which had won a prize was hung on the wall for exhibition, I was surprised that it seemed dull in comparison with the way it looked on the floor. It was on the third day that I discovered it was hung on the wrong side. The depth of color—a 3rd dimensional look—was on the right side whereas the wrong side had a flat look. That experience has convinced me more than ever that we should *not* lace on the right side of our rugs.

Years ago all rugs were finished with solid, dust-catching rows of black. A few individualists used other solid bands. Today, we may use blended borders as in "CHRISTMAS BELLS" or we may use a simple arrowhead in dark colors, but we forget about the black, and do not outline every few rows with a band of it. These concentric circles were part of every well-planned rug of years ago. The rug hookers all outlined each flower and leaf with black and the braiders made even greater use of what was then the commonest color to be found in the rag bag. We do give our rugs depth and a feeling of light and shadow by using several different shades of the same color, keeping our deepest values for the outer edge.

As for butting, methods have undergone radical changes, with a simplified one being used now which is half done when we start a braid with enclosed ends. In the chapter on butting, you will find several methods described which have been in use throughout the country over a period of years.

lacing

When the technique of "lacing" the braids with a cord came into prominence some years ago, it introduced a clever method of easing the tedious sewing and it has now been generally accepted as being stronger than the old sewing stitches. Years ago some women worked the third strand in their braids with a rug or crochet hook, and so joined their braids together without the help of thread or twine. Now by using narrow curved lacers or blunted darning needles and heavy lacing cord, much of the hard work of putting braids together has been eliminated and the time element shortened in an amazing way. I have also seen sail needles, long curved upholstery needles and short tapestry needles used.

Some of the lacers are flat and broad which may be all right for the wide braids, but the narrow, curved lacers or the blunted darning needles which will sew as well as lace, so that you can also use them for sewing the first two braids in your rug as well as for the lacing, are better for the narrow braids. Use whatever you may have or try one of the braidkins—you become accustomed to one very quickly.

For the new look in braided rugs, you can interlock your braids, with loops between loops instead of side by side. This gives an almost woven look to the rug and absolutely no threads show. The loops can be pulled together much more closely this way. When you start, tie a knot in your cord and hide it between folds. Do not skip a single loop on the straight sides of an oval or on a rectangle if you want a closely-made rug. If you do skip—and there are some who do it to speed the work—you will have dust pockets and your rug will not have body to it. Do not try to put the loops side by side. The surface will look more like one piece if the braids are tightly inter-locked, and when you add little patterns, they will be outstanding. Skip on the curves of an oval or on a round rug, but remember if you want a sturdy rug, *never* skip on straight sides. When you skip (or increase) for fullness on a curve, skip only one loop at a time or you will have a loose, floppy rug.

square knot

When we lace, we do so with a continuous thread. When we need a new piece, we simply tie a square knot and proceed, hiding the two little ends in a loop. Use about a yard of cord at a time. Anything longer will tangle and hamper your speed. To tie on a new piece, hold the old piece in the left hand, the new piece in the right, using thumb and forefinger. Put left over right and draw up. Now put right over left and draw up between the two loops. Hold lower ends taut with little fingers and pull top ends tight with thumb and fore-finger. (Fig. 7)

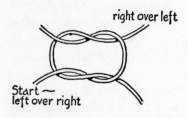

right over left

Start —
left over right

FIGURE 7

increasing on curves

Whether you want to make a round rug or an oval one, you must learn how to increase. This means that you are enlarging the outside curves. To do this, we skip a loop at a time on the braid which we are attaching—never on the mat itself. The only exception is in the making of some unusual rugs (see *decreasing*). There used to be guess work in the number of times we increased. The old rule of thumb was to increase just enough to always have the rug lie flat when it was lifted up and dropped. If you increased too much, the rug rippled; if too little, it buckled.

When we sewed our braids together, we did not count any stitches. When my mother would make little patterns along the straight sides of an oval, it was because she squeezed in the fullness along the ends at the curves. If the patterns came right on the second side, all well and good—they just happened.

It was an elderly woman who lived near Attleboro—Mrs. Georgia Cash—who pointed out to me that in lacing, we needed to increase three times only, since there are three strands in our braid, to bring back a design. Mrs. Cash found it hard to believe that anyone other than herself had ever thought of putting design into rugs. She put a great deal into hers. Moreover she squared her rugs with the straight braid and three increases at the corners, for she made only continuous braids—always beautifully small ones. From that one bit of information about the three increases, I have worked out many an unusual rug, not only for myself, but for thousands of eager braiders. Increasing in threes helps to keep the rug smooth and tailored, by keeping the colors against each other in the same position throughout a round. Three increases are made on *each* shoulder of a curve so there will be six around one full curve, no matter how small or how large the rug may be. If the rug seems too full, go around without any increases at all for one or two rows. Your designs will show up all around the curves. When you increase, these patterns are lost, but by keeping the skips on the shoulders, the middle ends will show the patterns. Put in T pins each time you make an increase to avoid having them come in the exact spot each round. Space them at different places or you will have points in your curves. When the rug is small, the increases will be closer together; as the rug grows larger, there will be more loops between the skips.

In making a round rug, it is better not to try to use design until the mat is at least 8-10 inches in diameter. Then we can increase more than we need for a round so that the rug does ripple. The next row will have no increases at all, with perhaps none in the row following. This is where you can make an arrowhead which takes only two rows, or the ric-rac which takes three rows to accomplish. If the rug still seems to ripple, use a wet cloth and a hot flatiron or a steam iron to press out. A little experience in this is your best teacher. When a round rug is about 12 inches in diameter, it will lend itself more easily to a novice for work in designs.

first bend in a rug

Who has not known the trials of trying to squeeze that first bend in a braid so it would lie flat and not hump up after a few rows had been put together? Today we braid that turn and the second one also, right into our oval or rectangular rug.

We use the modified square corner for the bends in the oval rug, to make the braid curve for us, doing it in this fashion. With the strand at your farthest left on the bottom, number them in your mind as 1, 2, 3. Put 1 over 2, 2 over 1 and pull 3 over tight. Repeat once and you have your first bend. Braid to the safety pin. Sew or lace these first two center rows. Repeat the modified square corner once, then braid two straight (four loops over each other which will accommodate the width of your braid if not over ¾ inch in width), and make the other half of your square corner on the second curve. Now your order of colors on the second side will be correct. This is the only time when you make these bends in this way. The rest of the rug will be braided with a straight braid. If you make your first bends this way, you will never have that humped-up look from which many rugs suffer. (Figs. 8, 9)

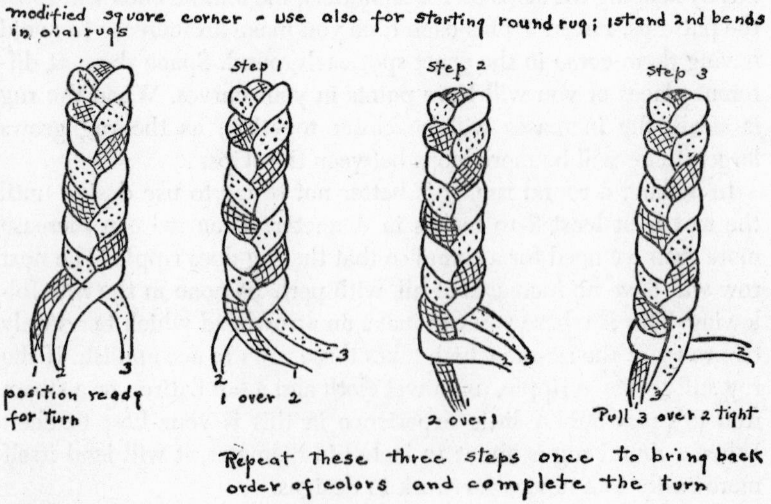

modified square corner - use also for starting round rug; 1st and 2nd bends in oval rugs

step 1   step 2   step 3

position ready for turn   1 over 2   2 over 1   Pull 3 over 2 tight

Repeat these three steps once to bring back order of colors and complete the turn

FIGURE 8

center of a round rug

Use the modified square corner about twelve times to form the center of your circle and you will always have a round rug which stays flat on the floor. Every one of my chair seats or round rugs is made in this fashion. The centers look like apple parings before they are sewn or laced together. I have yet to see one that wouldn't lie flat for me. It is just a little trick, but one well worth knowing and using.

First two bends
in oval rug

FIGURE 9

decreasing

When we make unusual rugs like "STARLIGHT" or "MERRY-GO-ROUND" or any rugs which have indentations and we want to bring back the shape, we can decrease by skipping a loop if there is no design to be considered, or three loops if there is a design, *on the mat itself*.

Sometimes a beginner finds her center is kidney-shaped. This is another place where we may find it convenient to decrease on the mat itself for a few rounds to take care of that indentation. If it is done gradually, it will come back into shape.

A scallop on a flower, a point on a star, the places between circles, can all be lessened as far as the shape goes by skipping in this way. In the latter type of rug, I like to skip three—one in the middle and one on each side. In making my octagon, the same procedure is followed.

These are the only times I skip a loop on the mat itself. If you do not decrease at these times, your rug will be rippling on the indentations and no amount of pressing will take care of it, nor will the rug have the shape you originally planned for it.

When you have braided over three hundred rugs as I have, you will have found many short cuts and ways for giving unique shapes to your mats and all sorts of original methods for working them out.

Perhaps you will be putting picot edges around the last row just as in an old rug found in western Massachusetts. You keep making inverted square corners for this to give you the little pointed edge. The modified square corner will scallop it; the sharp square corner picot it.

4

COLOR AND COLOR HARMONY
IN RUGS

If you have never been too conscious of color, interest in making a braided rug will awaken all your dormant appreciation of color in the world in which we live.

Here in New England, Mother Nature stages four perfectly arranged, different panoramas for us every year: the soft, grayed tones of sky and earth with delicate color of bursting buds as she comes to life in the spring; the lush, vibrant colors of sunny midsummer, tempered and cooled by the blue-greens of forest, lake, river and ocean; the gorgeous show which she flings over her hills in the autumn and covers with an azure sky; and finally, the cold, gray skies and drab fields of winter, with the deep evergreens turned gloomy sentinels in a world of dull colors.

As if Nature doesn't perform enough miracles for us, we now have beautifully colored pictures in our magazines which heighten our perceptions and teach us much about harmony and the effect of one color against another.

Color is a very involved subject, but we need only a simple chart, such as the one we remember from our school days, to remind us of the main principles which we must bear in mind if we are to make pleasing rugs. Our color wheel is marked off in solid lines with our primary colors of red, yellow and blue.

If we mix equal parts of red and yellow, we obtain orange; equal parts of yellow and blue give us green; while equal parts of blue and

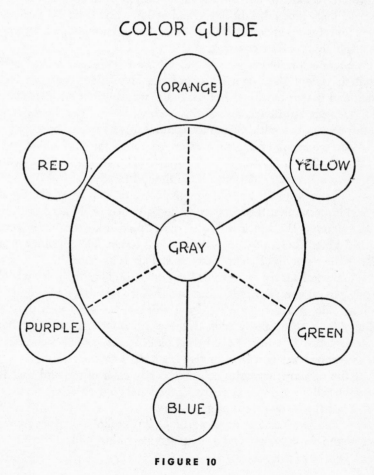

FIGURE 10

red give us purple. Orange, green and purple are called secondary colors. These and our primary colors are all strong hues.

When we see a rainbow, we see not only these colors but many soft shades of them because the sun, shining through the rain, grays them, and since some get more light than others, we have light and dark shadows. Our spectrum is made up of all these colors in their tints and shades.

Just as it would be difficult to live in a world where all these primary and secondary colors were used only in their full strength, so it would be hard to live with a rug so bright with scarlet, orange, purple, kelly green, bright blues, and yellows that it would seem to keep jumping up at you. A little of these strong hues goes a long way in brightening a floor covering.

We feel color. When we see red, we are emotionally stirred and excited; yellow gives us a feeling of sunshine; blues make us feel cool; and greens calm and rest us. But if we use these colors, not in full strength, but in weaker values which we may obtain by graying them, we can live with them most comfortably the year round.

When we speak of a certain *color*, we mean the *hue* which predominates. For instance, we speak of a red flower. It may be a deep pink or a soft rose shade, but it is in the red family.

When you are asked to change one color to another of the same *value*, it means that the hues are to be lightened or darkened in the same amount. We speak of "pale" pink, "pale" blue, or "dark" red, "dark" blue. These, of course, are general terms. The *intensity* of a hue is the strength of color it contains. This is its *chroma*.

When you hear the expression "Stay on one side of the color wheel when you choose your reds," it means that if you choose reds on the yellow side of the color wheel, you will not be using reds on the blue side—or the purply reds, as they are sometimes referred to. Often when bright scarlet and bright blue are put next to each other, the effect on the rug will be to give it a purple cast.

In the rainbow, opposite colors intensify each other, and that is why we call these opposite colors on the wheel our complementaries. With red the complement of green, these will both be intensified if put in the same braid or against each other in adjoining rows. As we see by the chart, orange is the complement of blue, and yellow is the complement of purple.

Pot of Gold

Colors next to each other on the wheel are analogous or "neighboring" colors. We create harmony through the use of these friendly relatives of the color wheel. Sometimes we pick up a color of the next group to accent our braids. When we use only neighboring colors on one side of the wheel, we say our rug is made with analogous harmony.

Often if a rug is in the wood tones with beige, tans, rusts, golds and browns used, the neighboring blue-greens are used to bring a feeling of coolness into these warm tones. Such a rug is "AUTUMN GLORY," which is tied together with tweeds and checks to help liven it in its setting of pine panelling.

Color, when used in room-sized rugs, should be grayed down considerably. More background tweeds and mixtures should be used than solid colors, for these tone down any strong values we may wish to use.

We may take one color, yellow, and work out our complete rug through its varying shades from all the yellow-beige tones to deepest browns as in "GOLDEN LATTICE," or for a warm room we wish to cool, we will use the blue-green tones. The materials for rugs like this should be dyed to insure blending of colors on the same side of our color wheel. Our droopiest mixtures will become the most interesting braids in the rug if we dye them, not in strong solutions but by putting 3 or 4 teaspoons of dye solution into our dye pot. It is just enough dye to color the very light threads of the mixtures.

Rugs worked out in several shades of one color are called monochromatic rugs and are often used with modern furniture.

Perhaps a few hints on the effect of color on the floor may assist those who are in a quandary as to what they will use.

Greens are recessive and will sink into the background. Sometimes we add a bit of bright green to our bronze-green dye to spark it, as it has a tendency to disappear especially when used with beige or gray mixtures. Gray-green, which we obtain by dyeing with reseda, has more depth over gray than over beige. Blue-greens, obtained through myrtle green or plain green or hunter green over gray, are easier to use than bright green, ocean or mint greens.

Blues used in too strong an intensity on the floor will stand out sharply if used in large quantities. Keep two strands of gray with it if you want to use it over a large area, or dye over gray.

Taupe will pull gray and tan together. Some commercial rugs in this color are called greige, pronounced *grayge,* and I consider it a wonderful background color. It is warm, yet recessive and restful, and where gray can take the life out of wood like maple, taupe will enrich it. With much taupe used in the wallpaper of the foyer where "TRANQUILLITY" is used, it is a perfect blend with the old rose into the mahogany and mulberry tones. The grays used in the rug were on the brown side, so the blue had to be well grayed in order not to be too obvious.

Instead of using yellows in a living room rug, try putting your beige mixtures into a gold dye bath. If the beige mixture has tan or brown in it, you will be much happier using the dyed material than the plain yellow. One woman who had used plain yellow was not at all satisfied with it, and took out many, many rows after I showed her a gold dyed mixture. After putting in the latter, she was completely happy. Old gold which tends toward a mustard shade is an excellent color for giving a sunshiny look to your rug without that "bedroom yellow." If you must use yellow, maize or aqualon yellow is not as harsh as a strong color like buttercup yellow.

Use of blue-grays will give a bluish cast, but remember that grays deaden maple furniture; for that use the yellow-grays. Beiges, tans and browns or mixtures with these colors in them enrich your rugs and give your maple or pine furniture or woodwork life and warmth.

Too much navy, brown or black in a rug can give a very flat look to it. Use these solid colors with tweedy mixtures to give the rug character.

Heed the colors which fall against one another. Juxtaposition can intensify strong hues to the point of overwhelming the rest of the colors used in a rug. Braids show quite an expanse of fabric in each fold. If you make small braids, individual loops are not so noticeable, but if your braids are large, be careful of the color combinations you put into adjacent rows.

Those who hooked rugs before they became braiders are apt to forget the large area of color shown in each loop of the braid. This is because they are accustomed to using such narrow strips of cloth in their lines of hooking. After a few rows of braiding, this point thrusts itself upon their consciousness, and from there on, they look at their work with a different point of view. Once this fact has been absorbed, they become excellent braiders, for they are well informed on color harmony, they know woolens and how to handle them, their eyes are trained to color, and they can visualize a finished rug which will have balance, unity and harmony.

We all interpret color differently. A "red" rose may mean varying shades to a group of people and so when a color guide is described in print, it may be interpreted in several ways. For that reason, it is much better to speak in terms of yellow-red, or blue-red, yellow-green or blue-green, so that one will have a definite guide for knowing which side of the color wheel is to be used. The words or description, "A red and green and beige rug," could mean a red shading to the purple or blue-reds or any yellow-green or blue-green used haphazardly. I've had this experience myself during that stage of my rug making when I did not pay so much attention to color or shades of color. Just finding the cloth was enough effort, I felt.

Next time you see colored pictures, look at the color blends and study them. It takes only a little practice to become color-conscious of everything in your life—clothes, draperies, floor coverings, wallpaper, prints wherever you find them. Notice the effect of one color against another. You will find your eyes are open to a new world of enjoyment. And your rugs will be far more beautiful because of this new interest and understanding of color.

5
PLANNING YOUR RUG

More people today are making room-sized rugs than ever before. The magazines are showing pictures of them constantly, some with settings of antique furniture or the reproductions which are so very popular today, and then again with the most modern furnishings.

Their nostalgic charm has captured the hearts of men and women all over the country, and this old craft is being plied as never before.

In planning a rug, consider first the room in which it will be used. Is it large or small, well-lighted and sunny, or dark and on the cold side of the house? What is the room used for and will there be children and pets using it? Your rug is to be one of the most enduring of the furnishings. You will change paint, wallpaper, draperies and upholstery more often than you will change your rug. So put into it the best of wearing woolens and colors which will be easy to live with over a period of years.

As a rule, a fair woman will want blues, a brunette likes reds, a redhead favors greens. Most men like reds.

A rug to be made for a living room with rich woods and traditional furnishings needs few colors, but it does need small braids, not over ¾ inch wide. The textures should be smooth, rich, velvety suedes, doeskins, broadcloth and close-clipped fleeces. Rugs made of these materials with fine workmanship can be used with orientals if the colors are rich tones and the materials are of plain fabrics.

A contemporary rug for casual living in a houseful of children, cats and dogs will live most happily with pine or maple furniture, and a braided rug of many, many tweeds dyed in various tones will make a soil-resistant background for the warm brown colors which will overspread your rug. If those flecks of white and beige in your tweedy mixtures are covered with a dye of gold, green or blue or terra cotta (which always ties in well with a brick fireplace), you will have a rug with overall charm and one which should be substantial and long wearing.

In a den, you may use your brighter colors if you wish but not so many as to be disturbing. As I write this, I smile to myself as I remember a pupil who made a rug for the den where her husband kept his collection of firearms. He was also a fire buff and had never lost his passion for chasing after fire trucks. She made him a rug of bright reds, gray tweeds and navy blue. It was a handsome rug with much design. She called it "BLAZE."

In making runners for dark halls, you can use lots of colors with your tweeds in almost every row so that they will not show tracking. Make your runners in long strips or in long rectangular form or make them with round circles put together with a few rows added all around to make the rug the proper width.

It goes without saying that a small rug in a large room will be lost, while the quieter a rug is, the larger it may seem in a small room without distracting anyone. If you want a lively, colorful rug in a large room with little furniture, it will lend personality and character in what otherwise might be a cold-looking, bare and cheerless room.

It has been said that a dining room should be a cheerful room, one which provokes pleasant conversation and a feeling of relaxation which in turn gives zest to the appetite and aids the digestion. Try to remember that the area at our feet as we sit around the table will receive the most wear, not only from our shoes but from falling crumbs. This is the place where you use your strongest cloth, both for wearing well and to keep soiled places from being too obvious. You may as well be practical when you are making your rugs.

If your dining room furniture is mahogany, you may wish to use soft gray aqua or turquoise blues, deep rose and wines with plenty of gray mixtures. The blue-grays will be fine here. These colors seem to enrich mahogany or walnut.

If the wood is cherry or maple, use beige mixtures instead of the grays for your background, with old gold, golden and spice browns, and highlight these not with the ordinary green but a blue-green. Or better still, if you can find a speck of turquoise anywhere in wallpaper, china or draperies, put a little into your rug for a truly out-of-the-ordinary rug.

Rugs for game rooms, family rooms, houses in the country or at the seashore can have lots of gay color. Use all your odds and ends and make hit-or-miss rugs if you like, using two strands of colors with one strand of plain background, or make wide bands of the three hit-or-miss strands between bands of planned color. These should be different widths, otherwise you will have them looking like so many of the machine-braided rugs which are on the market today. Hookers and braiders always have an accumulation of these odds and ends of materials in boxes and barrels. This is the time to use such pieces, and you can feel confident that they will make the right type of rug for such places.

Rugs for boys' rooms should be lively and bright with plenty of reds. You can use all the bright plaids you can find in such a rug, as long as the materials are sturdy. Mackinaw cloth is very good. I remember that I once had a bushel bag of bright-colored ski-woolens given to me. I was accustomed to making ½ inch-wide braids at the time, but I had to cut the ski-cloth wider to be sure the raw edges were hidden and it grieved me that I had to make braids which were ¾ inch wide. The rug was given away as a wedding gift. There are now four children in that household, so perhaps it is just as well that the rug was made of that sturdy ski-cloth.

Girls like reds also but usually toned down to pinks and rose. They like blues too, so make their rugs more on the pastel side.

"RAINBOW SPLENDOR," as its name implies, covers all the colors of the spectrum but in the weak shades. It was made for a guest room where it would not have too much wear. It is a beautiful rug, but it does take a lot of dyeing.

Plan small rugs for certain places. Made at random, you may find they will not fit anywhere when they are finished. A 3 x 5 foot rug is in good proportion and makes a sizable rug along the side of a bed. An 18-inch center makes a good scatter rug for in front of a bureau or chest. The 30 x 48 inch size is also quickly made and easily handled. Any rug with a center 18 inches to 24 inches makes a good size scatter rug, for the proportions will be right, whereas a rug made with a center under 12 inches will be a fat oval and should be avoided unless you are making it for a certain spot.

Square or round rugs are recommended for square entrance halls. If you have pretty new wallpaper or chintz, pick up your rug colors from them. Because rugs in your living rooms will be large, do not think you must pick up every color. Use just those you want to emphasize with several shades of these few colors.

"POT O' GOLD" is such a rug. This picked up colors from the chintz at the windows where it is used as well as from one chair. These are all pulled together with the browns with which the sofa is covered, and the gold is accented in the design to give sunshine to the room. Blue, the favorite color of the woman of the house, is used in the green-blue tones considerably grayed down. This is a rug in analogous harmony and is lively yet restrained, gay but not loud.

The same idea is used in "AUTUMN GLORY," where rusts are used instead of terra cotta, with the warm beiges, tans and browns cooled by the greens.

If you have odd-shaped rooms, plan your rugs to fit sections. They may not follow the same colors row for row, but they should be so related to each other in their outstanding colors that they will look well together in the same room.

A long narrow room might look better balanced with a large oval or rectangle in the center flanked by two smaller rugs for the two ends. In long rooms where one end is used for dining purposes, this has worked out very well in giving the illusion of a separate dining room. The three-circle rug has been popular for the center of a room with ovals or round rugs at each end. These center rugs can be worked out to measure 6 x 9 feet, which means that you start with three 12-inch circles. This can be worked out in a 9 x 12 also. Several two-wheel rugs have been made in the past few years but they seem to lack the balance of the three-circle rugs.

If you want a quietly beautiful rug, make a monochromatic rug in five shades of soft greens—using reseda dye for the gray-greens, or for the blue-greens, myrtle or plain green. Use your blended shades going from light to dark, making sure that you end the rug with your deepest values. This does not mean that you shade from light in the center to dark at the border by making only one gradation. You can go from medium to dark, then back to the lightest value and out to dark and so on. Sometimes it is not practical to start a rug with the lightest color in the center. Pick that up when the rug has a little size to it, so the light shades will not be massed together. Tans and browns can also give a good monochromatic rug, but they will naturally be on the warm tones.

You can set up a pattern for your rug as far as colors go in one-third to one-half of your rug, and if you like it, repeat it. Put it down on the floor where you are going to use it and step away from it just as a painter does when he works on his canvas. Try to envisage the whole rug as it will look when those rows have been enlarged and widened. Are there some combinations of tones which are too bold? Are there some which you wish you had made more often? This is the time to plan the balance of the rug, to maintain unity and repetition, to attain the balance needed to hold the rug down on the floor. If you have been working with the aid of a color guide, make any changes now which you feel are necessary to give you a better than ordinary rug. Pin on little triangles in different combinations to check any doubts you may have about certain groupings of color.

When you repeat your rug in thirds or fourths or halves, whatever the procedure may be, you may begin again with the combination with which you started the rug or go backwards with the color scheme. You can usually tell which you think is the better way. Much may depend upon the materials you have on hand.

If you plan to make a stair runner, think out one-half the width first. When you lace the opposite side, the colors will go on your safety pins in just the opposite way from what they did in the first half. Then the colors will fall against each other in the same position towards the center, and if you are making little designs, they will balance. If you forget to change the position of the strands, you will lose your balanced design.

You must measure and plan the entire length of the stair carpet so that you can buy enough material to do two sides or lengths instead of one. If you want the runner but feel you can't afford all that material by the yard, use several hit-or-miss rows for color, making sure to balance them on either side of the center. If you use plenty of strong tweedy mixtures, the runner will not show soil or wear as quickly as if plain colors are used.

You can work out your rugs or runners with crayons first, if you like, to give you some idea of your finished product. I like to work with the actual cloth, for with the small pieces of cloth pinned on a long strip, you can keep moving them around easily until you obtain just the results you wish. Over these combinations, staple a card with the number of rows you expect to make. If you have dyed, jot down that information for future reference. With the use of pins at first, you can place the scraps here and there to get the effect of light and dark, sunshine and shadow, and consequently will soon perceive where you may use contrasting colors for small designs.

The first braided rugs were planned with their concentric circles of black separating every few rows of color. We do not use much black today, but we do adhere to that old idea of setting off several rows with a solid band, sometimes two bands, even though the use of these solid bands tends to make the room look smaller. Complementary colored bands accent each other and do draw attention to the rugs, if nothing more. A woman in one of my classes some years ago made a rug in shades of beige, tans and browns. She accented them by solid bands of soft gold and turquoise, using these double bands three times in her 8 x 10 rug. The whole thing was butted of course, and was really stunning. The rug had rhythm, balance and unity as a result of this repetition.

If you are working up to a solid band in a continuous braid, the best method is to use that color—perhaps a green, first in one strand for a few rows, then in two strands for at least two rows, and then go into the solid green for a row or more. When you come out of it, use two strands for a few rows, then the one strand for a few rows. The greater number of rows you use with these combinations, the less noticeable will be the change from one color to another.

There is one thing which all who make braided rugs should avoid, especially in round rugs. This is a plain dark center. These form regular bull's-eyes and you keep having the feeling that you would like to try out a bow and arrow on it. Use a medium value for your center and use a mixture with two plain fabrics, or one plain and two tweeds, or three different colors. If you are a novice at braiding, you will grow very tired of working on a center which is all the same color. It can become deadly monotonous. I have had pupils, who at first insisted that they wanted a one color center, become bored and throw away what they had done and start anew with a more interesting combination of colors. Rugs should not have the effect that one such rug with a dark solid center had on a blind man. As he started to enter the room, he insisted that there was a hole in the middle of the room. He *felt* that dark center.

For your modern houses, the rugs may be monochromatic with a definite color used or they may be made entirely of tweeds. With modernistic furnishings, use odd shapes and big designs which will add a dramatic note. Let your rug be a conversation piece.

To a hooked and braided rug exhibit where I was to give a talk on present-day techniques in braiding, I took along with me a rug I called "CHINESE LACQUER." It was made with gold, old gold, rich blues, muted bronze-green tweed, and soft terra cotta mixtures. To my delight, one of the hooked rugs on display was one which had been copied in design and colors from an old Chinese rug in the Metropolitan Museum in New York. It was interesting to everyone there that in both rugs the same dyes had been used to gain certain colors. I had put designs in gold in mine, and there was much design in gold used in the hooked rug.

I once read that oriental rugs are remarkable because their designs are complex, subtle and surprising. Let us copy some of those ideas and design our braided rugs more skillfully.

6

"BUTTING"—OR JOINING
ROUNDS OF BRAID

"Butting" is the knack of joining together each round of braid so that it forms a complete circle and gives the rug a finished look with each row. This is in contrast with the continuous or spiral rug which is always just one long braid from the beginning to the end of the rug. Today even those who have always finished off their rugs with a tapered end have turned to butting for the last row or two, in order to obtain a more tailored finish to their rugs.

Butting may be done in several ways, and as you grow familiar with one method, it will seem easy until such time as you discover another method which seems smoother or one which saves time or cloth.

Here is a list of some of these techniques which I have known and tried out over a period of braiding in the past forty years:

1 This old French method used in Canada generations ago is still being used in some of the northern border states of our country. This consists of a tapered end followed by a strand started with a tapered end. This method is used in machine-made braided rugs. If the tapering is done too abruptly, a bulge will appear on the side of the rug where it is used.

2   I call this the "Maine method," for it is still used there in rugs made for the trade. Though I combed the countryside for years, I was never able to find any other method used to any extent. There is less lacing in Maine than any place else, and the women still laboriously sew their rugs on the wrong side with the over-and-over method. When the end is reached, the braids are pushed together with a few strong stitches to hold them in place. All but about two inches are cut off the ends. These are then thinned out and the material is folded back on each side and stitched down neatly. If the butt seems too high and clumsy, a wooden mallet or an iron hammer is used to flatten them.

I have had countless numbers of letters from Maine women who have told me they would not have believed it possible that they had butted rugs this way for so many years without having even thought of such a simple method as described in Method 7.

One must allow 6 extra inches of cloth for this process, and if the ends are not sewn down carefully, there will be bumps wherever the ends occur. A rug made with these joinings is not reversible.

The first time I made a rug with this type of butting, I was showing it to my young son, a most outspoken and honest young man. I told him I had made the rug for his room. I was crest-fallen, though not too surprised, at his reaction: "The colors are fine, Mom, and it's a pretty rug all right, but you put it in one of the other rooms and make me one without bumps so I won't stub my toes on them."

I tried to tell him that the rug would not be so bumpy when it had been used a lot, but he said he would take the rugs with continuous braids for his room—they were cozy and comfortable to walk on and presented no hazards. His reaction to the butted rug was my own and it led me to do a lot of inquiring and experimenting with other ways of joining rows.

3   My own mother spliced her ends and she also spliced when she added new color. The idea of wasting all that cloth and turning myself inside out as I labored over the joinings did not appeal to me. Perhaps a small pliers such as I find indispensable today in my work would have helped matters, but I worked, as she did, with a scissors and a crochet hook.

For this joining, one must leave 4 or 5 inches loose to work with, taper each strand in turn to a point, and then pull these through, one at a time, into the loop of matching color on the other end or beginning of the braid. It used to take me half an hour to make a presentable butt and I always griped over the extra cloth I had to throw away.

4   This is the method of starting to braid a new round rug with a very tight braid for about 6-8 inches. When ready to lace, leave about 6-8 inches loose so that when you are ready to join, the loose braid will be more pliable to work with. Overlap the two ends and mark with pins before you cut just where the joinings should be, matching color to color and cutting so that the seams will fall under the loops. Unbraid the tight beginning and rebraid with your usual uniform width.

Put Color 1 which you have cut (this will be the strand with which you started to braid) right side against right side and stitch. Turn to the right side and stitch along the side with a few blind stitches. Rebraid around this closed strand and join Strand 2 (the one on the opposite side of the braid from which you started) on the wrong side, blindstitching the side for a few inches. Strand 3 is the most difficult as the braid is now tight and there isn't much room for your fingers to braid the strands into position. Tweeds are much more pliable than hard-finished suedes. This third strand is the one which was in the middle, so if you use tweeds, try to remember to put the tweed in the center of your three strands when you put them on your safety pin. Be sure that Strand 3 is not twisted when you join the two ends. Ease the loops into position with your pliers.

This method gives an excellent joining, and if you have cut on a bias when joining your strips, there should be no bulk and no visible signs of a butt. It does take time and patience, but if you don't do much butting on your rug until you reach the last few rows, it is a good one to use.

5   This method is much like 4, but we do not start the braid any tighter than usual. It is best to draw the strand at your right over first when you begin to braid, and to have a material in the center with more stretch or give to it. Since it will be the last one to join, you will need to pull it so that the two ends can meet easily

when they are put against each other for the joining. In working this way as in Method 4, you must note the strand with which you start and cut that one first. You can put a pin to mark the spot to cut after you have overlapped the braids and decided where that cut should be. The longer the loose beginning of the braid and the end, the easier it will be to join these three strands in matching color.

In both Methods 4 and 5, remember that you will be unbraiding and rebraiding and that after the Number 1 braids are joined, you must braid around that strand. After the Number 2 strands are joined, Strand 3 must be pulled into position and stitched. If a little more length is allowed to the Number 3 strands, it will make the joinings easier. If they are too short, turn the ends in and blindstitch. Then sew together on the right side as you are doing the open folds. Watch the order of the colors on the sides of your braid when doing this method or Method 4, so that you will have the finished continuous braid in the same order.

6   This is the simple, well-liked and much used method of whipping over the three beginning ends of your strips with overcasting stitches. Leave about 2 or 3 inches loose as you start to attach a new braid. When ready to join, match the *order* of colors rather than the *colors* as you do in Methods 4 and 5. If the order of colors on the sides runs blue-yellow-tweed, it should be continued in that order throughout the round. This means that the tweed will go against the blue on one side and so on. The inside of your braid will have the same order and the colors should follow each other in the same way. Cut your cloth after pinning into position, overcast the ends as you did to the start of your braid, and sew together with blind stitches, keeping the braid the same width as in the rest of the rug.

If you have made increases in threes and because the butts are made near the shoulders of the curves, you can allow for extra fullness at this point and make a skip if you need to do so. The increases in threes help much in keeping the fullness exactly where it should be and the order of colors perfectly aligned for this butting.

7   This is the method which I use almost exclusively now. It lends itself to butting with bits of short braids when one wants to make

inserts such as letters or figures, and it is fast and neat and no materials are wasted. It is the fastest way I know of making a really acceptable joining. It is half made when you enclose the ends of your starting strands, for the method is just like Method 6 except that each strip is turned to the wrong side before you start to braid and stitched across the end and down the side about an inch. This may be done by hand or on the sewing machine, always remembering that hand-stitching is softer to the touch. You can overcast if you wish, but be sure to use matching thread.

Turn each strand to the right side with your small pliers, and push each seamed side back to the center of the strip. Your thumb will do it for you. String on to a safety pin with the open folds on the right and the nose of the pin pointing to the left. Braid your length. When you start to lace, you need to leave only 2 or 3 inches loose.

When you reach this place on your braid, match the order of colors on the sides and cut the strips with the contour of the braids—a *very* slight angle. The strand with which you started will be cut first, the middle one last and this is cut just a trifle longer than the others but not more than ⅛ inch. If you hold the braid with a T pin or a clip-type clothespin, it will not unbraid. After you have cut your ends, turn to the wrong side just as you did in the beginning, stitch across the top and down the side about an inch, use your pliers to turn back to the right side and rebraid. Sew across the end to hold, using matching strong thread and invisible stitches and keeping the braid the normal width. Milliner's thread is good. If you cannot find it, use double-duty thread which comes in all colors.

Finish the starting end the same way, and with a long thin darning needle, sew these two ends together with invisible firm stitches, sewing down the loops into place. When you have done this on the right side, turn over your rug and do it on the wrong side, so that the butt will be very neat on both sides. Never try to have one loop on top of another. Butting means "coming together head-on," and that is just what these ends are doing. The long needle is the key to a good joining, for it can reach back and forth under the loops as they are sewn together. The little pliers will be of invaluable aid in helping you to pull forward or back a loop which may be too long or too short. Look at Figs. 12, 13, 14 in Chap. 7.

This method of butting is done as easily on the rug as on a practice braid and takes only about ten minutes.

Butting is done by most New Englanders, but for those who are making their rugs for sale, the continuous rugs are faster. One rarely finds the combination of narrow braids and butted rounds being sold, for these take so much more time to make than the others that their price would be almost prohibitive if the time of the craftsman was considered. But the privately owned rugs here in New England and nearby states are beautifully made and so highly prized that it is almost impossible to find them even at exhibitions. The room-sized rugs are heavy to transport, and their owners usually feel they are taking unnecessary risks in allowing their prized possessions to be shown in strange places.

Well-butted rugs are constantly admired, for not a jog appears where new colors are added, and those who make them are unlimited in their designs.

Again, I repeat, butt at least the last row or two on every rug —you will be so happy with that finished look to your masterpiece.

7

THE ROUND RUG
OR CHAIR-SEAT

If you are advised to make a chair-seat as your first venture in rug braiding, don't lift your eyebrows and decide immediately that no one is going to force you to make one of those practice mats. You are going to start on a room-sized rug and nothing else. But if you are a beginner, you will save yourself time and money by making a small mat first, so why not let it be something usable like a chair-seat made out of old materials? Very little cloth is used in it, and if you have trouble in braiding, lacing or butting, you will not feel that you have ruined the center of a large rug.

Let's look at all the various techniques learned when you make a chair-seat. You make a modified square corner for the very center of your mat, so that it looks just like a one-piece apple paring before you start to lace it. Any round rug started this way will always lie flat because it is braided that way instead of a straight braid being coiled and squeezed into position.

You learn how to manipulate your first strands, how to make an even, smooth braid, how to tie a square knot in your thread which never comes out and gives you a continuous cord as a lacer. You will interlock your braids to impart a woven look; you will increase or skip, in the same way you do the curves on an oval rug, to make sure that your rug will always lie flat; you taper off the center the way many braiders taper off the end of their entire rug; and you will butt six or seven rounds of the chair-seat to give you good practice and make you adept in that important technique of braiding. You may even dye some of your old cloth and learn some tricks about a little design as you finish your last row or two.

A chair-seat may be small, but it is a wonderful project on which to learn techniques and it can grow and grow to all sizes and shapes if you want it to. (See what happened to "BOUQUET OF ZINNIAS," "CONTENTMENT," "MERRY-GO-ROUND" and "GOLDEN GLOW.")

A woman in Wellesley once used seven 12-inch circles, attached them in a straight row, surrounded them with eight rows of blended braids and had a fascinating runner for a long, narrow hall.

For the center of your chair-seat, you will need three strips of material, each about 54 inches in length. This will make your center from 5-6 inches in width if you braid a ⅝-¾ inch-wide braid and use woolens about 1½ inches wide. The center of a chair-seat is more interesting if it is made of two or three colors. If you would like a pinwheel effect like the center of "MINE ALONE," use two bright tweedy mixtures and one contrasting color in the third strand.

You can make either the T start or the "enclosed ends" to begin your braid, both methods being equally good. They are described in the chapter on techniques. If you use the enclosed ends, stitch across the end to hold and then slip back the safety pin if you have removed it in order to sew. Make sure that the pin's nose points to the left. Start to braid with the open folds either to the left or to the right, whichever is more convenient for you. Pull the right strand over first if it seems natural; if not, use the one from your left. Butted rows seem easier to join if the braid is started from the right, for then the last strand over has its seamed side toward the inside of the braid.

Pull the first strip over the middle, and the third one over the first. Put the middle one over the third. Now number them in your mind from left to right as 1—2—3. The strand at your farthest left is at the bottom.

Put 1 over 2, 2 over 1, and pull 3 over 2 tight. Repeat this process over and over until the tiny circle is about 3 inches in diameter. As you put it down, it curls into a circle of its own volition. Now that your center is all coiled for you, braid the rest of your strands straight. Before we come to the end, we must lace. We lace with the body of the rug away from us.

To lace, use about a yard of lacing-thread and your blunted darner. Put a knot in one end and hide in a loop at the center. You do your lacing on the wrong side of the rug, so push the safety pin over to the wrong side and lay your circle on a table. The first part of the center will be a sewing process so that you soon become accustomed to the work. You will lace after 3 or 4 stitches however, putting your needle (or lacer) between loops on one side of the mat and into the interlocking loops on the braid being attached. We never skip a loop on the mat itself—only on the braid being attached. At first, we skip every other loop on the braid, then every second loop and as the rug grows larger, we skip less. We lift the mat if necessary, to see where our lacer goes. We may also need to lift the braid being attached. We always work from right to left just as we sew. If you braid a very tight braid, you may like the blunted darning needle to do the whole rug for you. If you use a lacer, be sure to have one with a point, for it finds those openings in the folds faster than the wide flat lacers. Work clockwise so you can see what you are doing. Be sure to lace the coil right into the position in which it falls naturally.

As soon as you come to the straight braid, you will continue to interlock the braids, keeping each fold between the two on the adjacent braid. Pull your thread tight as you lace so that it never shows. If you can see it, push it back with your lacer. If it still shows, it is time to skip a loop.

The motion of the lacing is from the inside braid, down and up between loops on the adjoining braid. Put the needle down and draw up the thread each time between loops. Keeping the thread between the loops means that it is always concealed. Some people put the needle into two loops at a time when they wish to increase, but I feel the lacing can be much closer and that there is no strain on the thread if a loop is skipped entirely and pushed back into place with the lacer.

You will taper off your braid for the last 6-8 inches. If it were a larger mat, the tapered end would be longer. Taper gradually on each side of the three strands. (Fig. 11) Tuck these ends, one at a time in turn under each fold, with the last two turned over each other to simulate a braid. Use pliers, surgical scissors or eyebrow tweezers. If you have followed directions and been careful of your increases, you should have a well-rounded circle. Using heavy-duty thread to match, sew ends under the folds, cutting off ends which show, and overcast with invisible stitches. Do this to each one in turn.

FIGURE 11

If you do not like the shape of your center, snip threads in any bulging place and redistribute the fullness, using square knots to tie on and finish the new lacing. Pull the first lacing-thread through two or three loops and cut off. Blindstitch any raw edges of the tapered end which have a tendency to show.

In planning the next row, take into consideration whether you like this center well enough to make a rug out of it. If so, we must enlarge the center or it will be out of proportion to the size of a mat. Make another row or two just like the center, or use one or two of the same colors with others which do not show a complete jump into contrasting colors. This is the time to think about the future of your mat.

When I used to paint seascapes in oils, I used to say, "If I don't like this boat, I'll sink it." That was easy to do with a sweep of the paint-laden brush. But it is far more of a job to remove a few braids and replace them. It has been done in my classes, but I wouldn't advise it as ordinary procedure.

Let's enlarge our center gradually with blending shades of the colors we started with, if we decide that we do want a rug instead of a chair-seat. As a matter of fact, I like to make my first butted row just like the center, so that attention will not be drawn to the tapered end.

To start the first butted row, cut selvages off your three strips, turn to the wrong side and stitch close to the edges, along the end and down the side about an inch. With the pliers, turn to the right side, pulling out so that the end is straight across. With your thumbnail, push the open side (it is stitched so this is easy) back to the middle of the strand. Do this to all three strips, and push a medium-sized safety pin through the seamed side through all three strips, in turn, keeping the nose of the safety pin pointing towards the left. If you use braid-aids, be sure to slip them on before you enclose the ends. If you find it difficult to make the first few inches of your braid in your hands, run a strip of material through the safety pin between the top bar and the enclosed ends and attach this in the braid holder. It will hold the braid taut for you until you have braided a few inches. Square corners are best made in the fingers to insure the tight pull of Strand 3.

For this first butted row to go around your 5-6 inch-wide center, you will need a straight braid approximately 3 x 6 or 18 inches. Remember to check the sides of your braid occasionally to see that the colors are kept in the order you started with, red-gray-green, and that the folds are on the same side as they were when you started.

When you have made a braid long enough to go around, with 3-4 inches extra for the skips, lay the circle face down on the table with the safety pin on top. (Fig. 11) It is better to start the butted row in a different place than where you tapered off. If there seems to be a flat-looking side to your center, that is the place to skip once or twice to "full" it out. This is the row which takes care of any little discrepancies in the shape of your circle as you lace from right to left or clockwise, the nose of the safety pin towards you. If the open folds were kept at your left, they will now be facing you as you lace; if you kept them at your right, they will be on the inside of the braid which you are attaching. Leave 1-2 inches free as you start to lace on a butted braid. It gives you a little loose end when you come to butt.

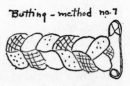

Butting - method no. 7

FIGURE 12

Tie a knot in your lacing cord and hide between a loop, usually about the 5th loop from your safety pin. Remember to interlock your loops and to skip often enough so that you do not see the threads with which you lace. If you skip in multiples of three, your colors will meet perfectly when you are ready to join the two ends. By leaving a little of the braid loose at the start, you can accomplish this in case they do not come together in the proper order, for you can, after joining them in the correct order, make one or even two increases. When you have laced to the end, put your braids together with order of colors matching to see where you will cut the strands. You want your braid after it is butted to look like one continuous round. Braid just a little beyond where they meet and turn to the right side. If you start to braid with the right-hand strand, that will be the first one you cut, the one on the left will be second, and the middle one last. This will face towards the inside of the braid if your folds have been kept on the right.

Godey Spray

If you braided with your folds to the left and if you started to braid from the left, the above will be just opposite: you will cut the left braid first, the right braid second, and last the middle one which will face towards the left.

As you cut these, (Fig. 13), allow only enough seam for overcasting, and cut on the contour of the braid, a very slight bias. Do this to your next strand. The last strand is cut just a trifle longer than the others.

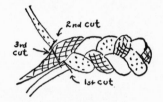

FIGURE 13

If you put a clip-type clothespin in your braid to keep from unbraiding, you will save yourself a little extra work. When you have cut all three, turn each strand to the wrong side and as in the beginning, stitch or overcast across each end and down the side about an inch. Turn to the right side with the pliers and rebraid. With strong matching thread, stitch across end to hold. Do the same to the other end. Now butt together head on, so that order of colors is maintained and stitch through under the loops from one end to another, until the two ends are joined carefully. Turn to the other side and take care of any loose ends. Milliner's thread is very good for this purpose, or double heavy-duty thread if you cannot find the other. If one loop seems too short, use the pliers to pull it forward into place. If too long, pull it back a loop or two. (Fig. 14)

Now finish the lacing. If you butt your rugs, you will probably want to use the blunted darner for lacing, for this will do all your work except the stitching for the ends, and it will go through the butts easily on each row. Always, when making a chair-seat or a round rug, have the butts come at spaced intervals around the rows.

Each successive row is started at a different place, and each braid will be three or four inches longer than the preceding row. If you would like a design, make enough skips in the first row to allow you to have one or two rows of clear pattern without any skips at all. If, after you have butted on six or seven rows and the mat is complete but still ripples, turn it to the wrong side and using a very damp cloth and a hot iron, press and leave flat until dry. You can always iron out small troubles. If your braids are of uniform width and you have laced properly, any rippling or hooping can be found in too much or too little increasing.

FIGURE 14

If you prefer another method of butting, use it by all means. But if you want to make letters or figures or flowers in your braids, you will find this method the easiest to use. Figures 12, 13 and 14 may help you to understand any of the fine points of butting in this fashion.

8

THE OVAL RUG

In making the ever-popular oval rug, you can make a continuous or spiral braid, tapering off the next to the last row or two, and then finishing your rug with one or two butted rows, like "HARMONY." Or you may want to butt each row from the start as "AUTUMN SUN-SHINE" was made. Or you may like to use the method which I find most satisfactory: make the center section, taper it off and butt all the remaining rows, as was done in "COUNTRY KITCHEN."

Making a continuous or spiral braid is the fastest, but you should know a few tricks which, combined with a little thought, will keep your rug from showing unsightly jogs where the new colors are attached.

Rule 1 on the list is to have plenty of tweedy mixtures, checks, plaids, mixtures of all kinds to act as background colors for your rug. They will tie in your solid colors when you are making changes, especially if you put a weak dye over them of the same color you want to pick up in the following rows. Many of the neutral shades help in this way also. For example, if you are going from grays, blues or greens into browns, taupe will bridge the gap.

Rule 2: After you have decided what you want for distinctive colors, make out a color guide to see how you want them placed in your rug, either for a blending harmony or for complementary contrasts.

Rule 3: If the rug is for yourself and not being made for sale, make narrow braids. Don't rush your rug with wide braids; it is no marathon you are taking part in. Far better a beautifully constructed rug which will be an heirloom than something which will be falling apart in a few years.

Let's see how much material we need to buy for a rug. A round rug will need less than an oval, and an oval less than a square-cornered one of approximately the same size, for we have no corners to think about. Because of the fact that tweeds will have more pull or give to them than the hard-finished, closely woven fabrics and varying weights as well, these figures will necessarily vary.

Assuming that we use about ⅝ of a pound of cloth to a square foot, a 2 x 3 ft. rug will weigh about 3 or 4 pounds. A 3 x 5 ft. rug will weigh between 7 and 9 pounds. This is one of the most popular-sized scatter rugs made, and you can plan about 4-6 pounds of background materials, with 2 pounds of the predominating color and about 1 pound each of two or three secondary colors to blend or accent.

For a 6 x 9 ft. oval, you will need about 30 pounds. For an 8 x 10 ft. rug, plan on close to 45 pounds and for a 9 x 12 ft. rug, you will use from 60 to 70 pounds.

As no two people braid just alike, for the reasons given above, these amounts are merely a guide and not the exact amounts of materials you will use. If you buy headings by the pound, allow 20% for waste and do take into consideration the fact that all the materials may vary as to weight.

If you use 1½ in.-wide strips for your braids, you will be able to tear 24 strips from a yard of cloth, making sure that you tear from selvage to selvage. If the material is the hard-finished kind with a pile, such as a suede or a fleece, tear it into 1¼ in.-wide strips to work out with the 1½ in.-wide tweeds or flannels. This will give you a ¾ in.-wide braid for your rug.

I always say to beginners, "Make a tight braid" so they will be sure to make a firm braid. I have found only two women who braided so close that it seemed as if they took the very life out of the wool. After all, wool is taken from a live animal and it has a good deal of resiliency even after it has been woven into cloth. Let's leave some in it to give springiness under our feet as we walk upon our rugs. We are trying to get away from the hard feeling of boards or stone when we cover up our floors.

As we learned when we made a chair-seat, three lengths of material from 54-60 inch-wide materials the ordinary widths of woolens, will braid into a length from 36-40 inches, depending upon the closeness of weave and the tightness of your braid.

If you want a rug that looks long, make a narrow center; if you want a wide-looking one, make the center wider than you ordinarily would. A 9 x 12 ft. rug should have a center which measures at least 12 inches or more across.

When I mention rows, I refer to double rows, of course, to give the rug perfect balance. All rugs should be made with this even number on each side of the seam where you put the first two rows together. Balance is one of the essentials of good construction.

"How do we determine the length of the center braid?" This is a question often asked by the uninitiated. For an oval or a rectangular rug, we think in terms of the finished rug. What size do you want your rug? What is to be the difference between the length and the width? That will be your starting length. If you want a 2 x 3 mat, start with the difference between 2 and 3, or 1 foot—12 inches. You would start a 3 x 4 ft. or a 4 x 5 ft. rug each with 1 ft. or 12 inch centers.

A 2 ft. length will make you rugs of 2 x 4, 3 x 5, 4 x 6, 5 x 7, 6 x 8, 7 x 9, 8 x 10 ft. and so on. A 3 ft. center length will make 3 x 6, 4 x 7, 5 x 8, 6 x 9, 7 x 10, 8 x 11, 9 x 12 rugs.

One day when I was looking over remnants in a mill store, I overheard the conversation of two women, one of whom was making a braided rug. In reply to her friend's query about the size of her rug, the braider answered, "Oh, it's three feet now."

""How long is it?" was the next question.

"Just the same—three feet," was the answer.

"But I thought you were making an oval rug."

"I am," was the response.

"But how can it be an oval if you started with a circle?"

I held my breath, thinking I might have hit on something new. "Because I want it to be," was the determined reply which let me down completely.

"I don't think you can do that," said the first. Then she turned to me. "Do you braid?" she asked, and when I replied in the affirmative, "Do you think she can turn her round rug into an oval?"

I thought fast. "Perhaps she is going to make a two or three circle rug," I suggested.

The braider glared at me. "I'm making an eight by ten oval," she said flatly and finally.

I was either mean or kind—I have never been able to decide which —for I said as gently as possible, "Then you should have started with a two-foot center, or the difference between eight and ten feet."

She looked dubious. "Have you made many rugs yourself?" she asked me.

"Many," I replied, "and I teach rug braiding to hundreds every year."

With that, feeling guilty and somewhat ashamed of speaking so bluntly, I left without completing my purchases. Perhaps she didn't believe a word I said and for all I know, she may now have a fine big round rug which makes her completely happy.

Having decided on the length you are going to make your center, select three strips of varying lengths so that there will be no seams coming together to make any bulk in your braid, and enclose the ends as you did with the butted rows for your chair-seat. If you use the braid-aids, slip them on before you enclose the ends, then push them down a little ways while you turn your materials to the wrong side and stitch along the ends and a little way down the side of each strip. When you turn these ends to the right side, be sure that you have the ends straight across and not in points. Pinch in the seamed sides and string on a medium-sized safety pin with open folds to the right.

If you find it difficult to start the braid in your fingers, put a loop of cloth like any of your strips under the top wire of your safety pin and catch the two ends in your braid-holder. Your pin will have its nose pointing to the left. Start to braid with the fold on your right, swinging it over the middle. Now swing the one on the left over the one which is now in the middle. In turn, the one on the bottom is swung around the side over the top. Braid firmly, and see that your loops are always close together. Keep loose ends tucked in with thumbs and forefingers if you do not use braid-aids. If you are using them, check the wrong side of the braid frequently to see that the folds stay on the right edge and do not slip around to the back or slip so that the raw edges are showing. The braid-aids are just what their name implies but they are not expected to do everything for you. See that your material is heavy enough so that you do not have to line it when you are using these aids, or else have it so wide that it can be well turned in for extra thickness. If you do not watch for this, you will have those tweaks or creases about which I have warned you.

If you braid properly, you will always have your thumbnails in sight. Watch that point so that you do not turn over the cloth and plait instead of bringing it around the sides and braiding.

Suppose you are making a 9 x 12 ft. rug. Whenever we measured for that center, we used to allow an extra inch for the turn. We do not need to do that now. Measure carefully, not pulling the braid at all, and when you have a full 3 ft., remove the braid from the holder, and make a modified square corner, twice in succession, to turn that first bend. This is the same technique with which you turned the center for your chair-seat. With the strand at your farthest left on the bottom, number them in your mind as 1, 2, 3. Put 1 over 2, 2 over 1 and pull 3 over tight. Repeat once and now braid straight to the beginning of your braid. Note how the two braids cling together. They will fall into the position in which you will attach them, and they will always lie flat. No more humping or pressing to stay down.

Before you start to attach the braids, sew the three strands together at your safety pin end. Do not pull them together into a point, just leave them the same width as the rest of your braid, as you learned to do when you made those butted rows for your chair-seat If you are careful, you need not remove the safety pin. If you do, put it back in the same position, for it is a guidepost to many of your techniques. Keep it on the *wrong* side from now on.

When we attach the two center braids, we find the process a bit more difficult than merely lacing, for they "march" in opposite directions. We can start at the pin and lace every other loop to the bend; then coming back, we can pick up and lace the loops we skipped; or, as I like to do now, start at the bend with a blunted darning needle and heavy lacing-cord, make a knot, and attach by sewing through the cloth, away from you and lacing towards you. The two braids are lying with the right sides face down on a table, safety pin on your left. You sew and lace clockwise, always with the light over your left shoulder as you work, so you can see where you are working. Lace with the body of the rug away from you. Be sure to go through the fabric as you sew away from you, and do not lace back in the same spot, but always move your needle a little towards the left. With the two braids clinging together, notice, as you start this process, the colors which naturally stay together and keep them this way through the entire length. They are not side by side but interlocked as if woven. Keep all your lacing that way.

When you reach the safety pin, you will note where you need to make another modified square corner for the second bend. As soon as you have made one turn, you must braid the next two loops in the usual way to accommodate the width of your braid. Now make two turns from the left to finish the corner; the rest of the rug is straight braiding. As soon as you have sewn around this end where your safety pin stays, you will be able to lace in the usual way, interlocking each loop on the sides of your rug without any skips, skipping (increasing) only on the curves. (Fig. 8)

If you have attached your center firmly, you will find it is absolutely straight and you have kept the same colors throughout. Now when you lace, you will keep the same colors interlocked between each other and the sides will be kept straight. Pull the thread firmly and closely between loops so that it does not show. When you reach the first bend, you will need to increase in the six loops which form the tiny curve. Be sure that it *is* six so that the pattern made by keeping the same colors between each other will be the same as on the opposite side. When you reach the next curve, you will make three increases, braid one straight and skip three more.

Note that we skip a loop completely when we increase. I think the increases are much smoother if we do not try to go into two loops at once. Skipping a single loop is not such a strain on the thread and we can pull our thread tighter. If you keep T pins where you increase, you will be able to space them more easily. At first there is 1 loop between them, then 2, 3, and so on. But if the pins are put in directly, they can act as a guide in making symmetrical curves. You will not be putting them in the same places and then finding that you have points in the curves. You can also turn your end curves over on each other to make sure they are alike. Treat them as halves of a circle.

The reason we increase in threes is that our braids are made up of three strands, so the order of our colors comes back after the third increase. It is lost while we are increasing. If you are careful always to put these increases on the *shoulders* of a curve, leaving the ends free, any little designs which you may be putting into your rug will be plainly seen on the ends as well as on the two sides, and the larger the rug grows, the farther apart these increases will be spaced. If at first six skips around a whole end seem too many and the rug appears a bit full, use a cloth wrung out of water and a hot iron to press on the wrong side.

When the rug is larger and seems too full, go around with no increases for a couple of rows while you put in design. This will flatten out your ripples. If the rug starts to ripple on the sides, you are probably making a larger braid than the ones in the previous rows. This is a common fault, particularly in group work where everyone is so ambitious. If one or two work a little harder and forge ahead, the others will try to catch up in a hurry, with the result that braids are apt to become a little larger and lacing a bit looser, and the whole rug suffers.

If you want a diagonal effect in your center, start with two strands of the same color with one contrasting braid, and keep the same colors interlocked between each other until your center is finished. (See "GOLDEN LATTICE.")

By keeping the T pins in for markers, you can readily see where you will finish your tapered end. This always comes on the curve where the safety pin points, and we start to taper for the last 10 inches or so. Each row completes its curve on that shoulder and the three ends of your row should fit into the loops where that last increase is nearest the straight side of the rug.

Having tapered off as you learned in doing the center of the chairseat when you cut each side of every strand until it tapered into practically nothing, tuck them one at a time in three successive loops, stitch in place with matching thread, cut off surplus cloth, and overcast with tiny invisible stitches.

Having completed the center this way, all the rest of the rug will have butted rows.

If you have been careful about your work, you will have a symmetrical oval, but if there are any minor troubles, perhaps the next row can take care of them. Use the same combination of colors which you used in the preceding row for it. If you used one each of three different colors, use two of one and let the other be a contrast. You can form an arrowhead design with this combination and if the place you tapered off is not quite as symmetrical a curve as you would have liked, this row will, no doubt, fix it up.

If you have a kidney-shaped center, the chances are that you skipped a loop on the side or that your braids were uneven or that you laced close together in some places and loosely in others. If you made a chair-seat first, you should be making a uniform braid by now and you should be lacing with an even tension.

Start the butted rows with ends enclosed, as you started your first butted braid for a round rug, and if you want a neat butt or joining of the two ends, start to braid with the strand at your right, so that the last strand to be turned will be toward the inside of the braid, and so less noticeable. This is always the hardest one to do.

Start your first butted row at the other end of the rug, always at the beginning of the shoulder curves, never on the straight sides. Such rows are less conspicuous at the shoulder ends, and should go from one side to another in turn, so that they come once in four rounds at the same curve, though always a bit off a straight line. (Fig. 15)

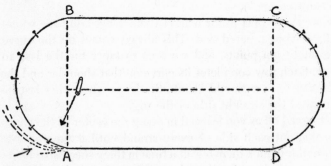

A ~ end of tapered finish
    Butt just above ABCD
    Change color just above A at arrow

FIGURE 15

When you are making a large rug and have a limited space in which to work, keep the rug rolled and as you put on the butted rows, work with four rows going at once. This is very helpful in a husband-and-wife team of which there are many. Since the wife invariably does the butting and the husband is always calling for more braids, a solution to the problem may be in having three or four of these braids being attached at once. When a woman has to lift a heavy rug up on a table, she may as well make it worth her while. As a working space, two folding card tables do nicely.

If your oval rug is to be a continuous braid, you will change your colors on the same shoulder where you tapered off for a butted rug. This can be remembered through the constant use of the safety pin.

When ready to change a color, braid just a little beyond the place where the change will come, and making sure that the new color will come on the outside of the braid, mark with a pin (Fig. 15) the spot which is to be cut. Make the cut on the bias from upper left to lower right, like the contour of the braid. In this way, your new color will fall just right. Do not allow too much for a seam and be sure to press that seam open with your thumb so there will be no bulk at the spot. If it is necessary to change two colors at the same time, do one right after the other. When you attach this new piece, open up the strand to its full width before you try to sew on the new piece.

When changing from one color to another, try to use the same values. The change is less noticeable. When working up to a solid band, use the old rule of 1, 2, 3, 2, 1. This means that if you have one red in a row, the next row will have two red and the next one three red, and going away from the red, we have two in the following row and finish the red with one strand. If you want the change even less noticeable, make several rows of each combination except for the one solid row. The more rows there are of the same combinations, the less apparent are any jogs.

Using a mixture with these blending bands can be of great assistance. The light mixtures make a contrast with any solid color and allow the use of many designs since they tie the other solid shades together. If, as has been already suggested, you use a weak dye of your solid colors over them, they act as an even better tie-in in successive rows.

The question has often been asked of me as to what I would do if pressing a rug did not take out the kidney-shape of the center. Could there be any other solution than ripping out the whole thing?

Yes, we can try wider braids and looser lacing at that indentation, and on the opposite side, we can skip a loop on the rug itself. We may need to repeat this on two or three rows, but if the trouble is not too pronounced, a "reef" taken in this manner may straighten out your sides. If when you press, you can tack the rug into shape and leave it over night under a wet cloth, it may stretch and pull the wool into shape. If none of this helps, rip it out and start fresh, observing all the rules carefully. Make sure that you braid with an even width. If your materials are of different weight, you must allow for that point when you cut or tear your cloth. Torn cloth has a softer edge and is easier to turn in with your fingers. Sometimes you will need to cut 2-2½ inches wide on worsteds, to give them bulk enough to use with fleeces, heavy shirtings and coatings. Worsteds and tweedy mixtures are usually torn or cut wider to equalize strands for the same braid. A little practice and you will be able to use many different woolens with different weights and thicknesses in the same rug. Some materials must be turned into thirds; some doubled and redoubled.

The chair-seat will teach you much about fabrics and how to handle them. So choose one as your first project before you start your large rug.

The "new look" in braided rugs is due to the interwoven appearance the lacing gives. But don't jeopardize the life of your rug nor the smooth looks of it by skipping loops on the straight sides for the sake of speed. If you do this—I have seen some rugs made by skipping every other loop first on the mat itself and then on the braid being attached—you will cause dirt pockets and shapeless braids.

If, as you lace, you will lift the braid being attached, your lacing needle will slip from one side to the other very easily and you need to pull up the thread tight with only every three or four loops. Do this on the wrong side of the rug, and if you lace clockwise or right to left, the braiding will be done with no loss of motion.

I like to hide any ends of thread left after making square knots as soon as I have laced a few loops. It keeps the rug looking neat, and while the rug is small, it is convenient to turn it over and check on those loose ends going between the loops onto the other side.

Many people still like to sew their rugs because they think being sewn on the wrong side allows the right side of the rug to have more depth to it. I quite agree about the depth, but we who lace can have the same effect if we will lace our rugs on the wrong side. The side on which we lace is the flatter-looking surface. The right side, with its different textures due to the pile on some of the materials, will have depth similar to our orientals and domestic rugs. If the braids are small, they will also have a smooth look, not a flat look but a tailored one, for every loop is interwoven with its neighboring loop. We can have elegant smooth-looking braided rugs if we wish, made of suedes and broadcloth, but let's not overlook the fact that rug-braiding is a homespun craft. We don't want our rugs to look machine-made. We want to feel that springiness under our feet that gives us a sense of warmth and cheerfulness.

If you are making rugs for sale, try to have a good place to work so that you will not need to remove all your materials and rugs every time a meal is to be served or visitors come into the house. If at all possible, have a room where you can drop things in a hurry and let them stay put until you return. I work on a ping-pong table when I do the large rugs, but some women I know have a better plan. They have set up two saw horses supporting long pieces of plywood. As I have with my table, they have covered their plywood with heavy brown paper, thumbtacked into place. This allows the rug to be pushed around easily. A sturdy wooden chair on which to sit gives the most satisfaction. An upright holder can be moved along with your chair or the rug will slide around to you. If you have an empty bedroom, that should be an ideal place to work. One woman I know works in her attic, another in her basement. I have worked all over my house, depending on my project. A single card table, a double card table, and a flat sewing board, 3 x 5 feet, which I was fortunate enough to pick up from a former dressmaker, all seem to take turns in my little sitting room. I prefer working there to my basement workshop.

If you keep your large rug on the floor as it is being made, try to find a high Victorian footstool, with casters if possible. This allows you to roll along as you work. You can hold a piece of plywood or masonite on your lap. All rugs should be laced on flat surfaces. This is much easier for me than working on my ping-pong table when I am lacing. With the rug flat, I can keep the whole thing in view as I lace on four butted rows at a time. Of course any footstool will do, but some are so low they can be quite uncomfortable.

If you are in doubt as to what kind of a rug will look best in your rooms, try an oval first; it fits most anywhere. You can make the unusual ones later when you have more confidence in your own ability as a braider.

9

SQUARE-CORNERED RUGS

Square-cornered rugs have been made for years, but today with our new and improved techniques, we are making squarer corners than ever.

When rugs were sewn, they were put together in straight strips and a few butted rows were then attached, with the extra fullness squeezed in at the corners. That was your square-cornered rug. If the rug was not put together in strips, it was worked out as a "squarish oval" with the corners squeezed in full to give the rug a squared look.

When lacing came into vogue, it simplified matters for the braiders, for now we could make three consecutive increases at the corners to square a rug. "BLUE DIAMONDS" is a rug squared in this fashion. It gives a slightly rounded effect and a gentle curve to the ends which some people find more graceful than the sharper corners.

I have learned much from my pupils' mistakes, but never did I expect to learn so much as I did from the continuous mistake made by a man in one of my classes. He was learning to braid and he kept twisting his braids twice from the left before he pulled over the one from the right. When I took the braid from him to see if I could discover the reason for the twists in his braid, I realized that a squared corner had been made. With a little experimentation, I found that if I repeated the same kind of turn twice, the order of the colors on the side came back into place. I worked over this idea and found that if the strand at the left was turned over three times before pulling over the strand at the right, the order of colors came back and a much squarer corner was formed. Only one thing was wrong about this. I tried it out with my classes and invariably the strand at the right was not pulled tight enough, with the result that there were holes all along the diagonals of the rug. I went back to the "two and two over" method in my work with my classes, but made my own rugs with the sharper corners. Now I use it almost exclusively. The difference is most noticeable. And because the idea of squared corners is now some five or six years old as far as I am concerned, it is easier to teach and many of the experienced braiders have taken up the idea wholeheartedly. The novices are still intrigued when they see me do it. The thousands of men and women who crowd about me each September to watch me demonstrate at the Springfield, Massachusetts, Eastern States Exposition come especially to see the square corners turned in both the modified and the sharp turns. They have told me time and again that making their first bends in an oval rug lie flat through the use of the modified square corners, and the application of that same technique to the round rug so that the rug will never hump up in the center, are the two best new ideas which have been introduced into braided rugs in years.

As far as the square-cornered rugs go, I told of two kinds in *Let's Braid a Rug*, my booklet published in 1954, for I did not think the public would be receptive to the sharp square corners. In my groups of teachers, however, the latter was taught, and now I can safely say that it is the method most commonly used. It certainly is the easiest to lace, for that strand at the right which is pulled tight, is the only one which is skipped as you lace.

Though the directions for making the modified square corner have been given to you in the directions for making the center of your chair-seat, they are given again here in case you want to make a square-cornered rug as your first venture in braiding.

You will of course enclose the ends in the usual way, not forgetting to slip on the braid-aids first if you use them. The open folds are at your right. Braid the length you need for the center. Now number your strands from left to right: 1, 2, 3. Turn 1 over 2 as usual. Now turn 2 over 1 and pull 3 over tight. Repeat once with the new order of colors, 1, 2, 3. 1 over 2, 2 over 1, and pull 3 over tight. You have turned a modified square corner and the colors on the side of the braid are in the original order. (Look at Fig. 8) Braid and lace to the next corner. Make the turn again. Braid two turns of straight braid and make another double turn. If you call it double instead of just a turn, you will remember to make the turn twice, otherwise it will not be a square corner and your original order of colors will disappear and if you are making designs, you will lose them.

The straight braids between corners will increase in number as each row is added. You can count them if you wish, to make sure the rug is being squared in the correct spot, or easier still, you can have a safety pin at each end of your center and one in the middle. When you are ready to square, turn the end to the center to check the correct place where you are making the corner.

For the *sharp* square corner which I now use all the time, I number the strands as usual from left to right: 1, 2, 3. This is done when the one at your farthest left is on the bottom. Put 1 over 2, 2 over 1, 1 over 2, and pull 3 over 1 tight. Do this only once and you have a sharp square corner. (Fig. 16)

pull tight

3 turns from the left once

FIGURE 16

Of course for the first turn in your rectangle, you need to do this twice in succession because there are two corners. When you come to the next corner, make the turn once and then braid two loops straight. This will allow for the width of your single braid. You should attach the two center braids before you make these square corners to be sure that you make them in the right loops.

When you have sewn around this second square corner, the rest of your rug will be laced. Remember *to always skip* that loop which you pulled tight from the right—even from the start of the braid. This will keep a good corner and allow the loops to fall into the correct position on each side, and will preserve the continuous pattern with which you started.

As your rug grows, keep turning the ends towards the center to check the corners. If the rug is inclined to go outside, you may be squaring too soon. If the corners tend to bend inward, you should have increased sooner. This is the time to correct your corner before you go any farther with your rug. Braiding in your corners this way means that your corners must be true with each turn, or the whole rug will soon be askew.

The rug is ended where that first safety pin points, at the beginning of the braid. Taper gently for only a couple of inches and tuck the ends into the corner loops, stitch under, cut off excess material, and overcast with invisible stitches and matching thread.

These rugs lend themselves beautifully to continuous braids and designs with the new color being added in the middle increase or, if that isn't convenient, in the loop below it. Have the new color come on the right side first. Mark the spot with a pin, unbraid a bit, and cut the strip on a bias from upper left to lower right. If it is necessary to make two changes, make one right after the other.

You can always butt these rugs as I have in "APPLE BLOSSOM TIME" and in the rugs with hooked centers. The stair treads are continuous except for the last row or two. I find the continuous ones just as acceptable as the butted ones, for the new color changes are far less noticeable in the corner diagonals of a squared rug than in an oval.

If you want to make a perfectly square rug such as "DOMINO," start with sharp square corners at once, making four of them. Lace at once, so you will know exactly where to put your turns and how many straight braids come between each corner. Keep your pin pointing towards the first corner so you will remember where to add new color and where to end your rug. Only one pin is necessary for you keep turning the ends to each other if in doubt as to the shape of your square rug.

In all your square rugs where you braid the shape into your strands, you must braid only what you think is the correct length for a side, then lace it on, so that you do not go beyond the corner and have to take out some of your work. Keep your mind on the length you are making so you won't be wasting your time making extra braids.

If you are making square-cornered rugs with three consecutive increases at the corners—this means you square as you lace—you can braid well in advance of your lacing. These square corners have one real advantage. If, as the rug progresses, it seems to be a bit lopsided as far as the corners go, you can snip the threads and change them to form more perfect diagonals. I have seen this done many a time.

In continuous braids, be sure to check on your designs when you add a new color at the first corner. You may need to change to a different color than the one you had planned on, or you may need to skip an extra loop to arrange your pattern. This will throw off your diagonals. So plan your changes gradually and avoid any skip in the sharp-cornered rug.

If you are going to make any unusual rugs, you need to know how to make both the modified and the sharp square corners. In making letters or figures in a rug, both of these methods are used. You can invert the turns, putting them on the right of your braid instead of the left. These inverted square corners are used in "MERRY-GO-ROUND," "STARLIGHT," "GOLDEN GLOW," and others.

There are endless possibilities to the rugs which can be worked out with these turns. I once planned to work out a Maltese Cross and a little red schoolhouse. It can be done but what I lack is that "ever-fleeting" time. There are always so many who want to learn the little tricks which I have already worked out. It is the same story with so many of our brain children—there just aren't enough hours in a day.

Perhaps in a few years, I shall see little red schoolhouses springing up in many a rug exhibition as well as my Maltese Cross and lots of little animal rugs and many things I haven't even thought of. It is high time that modern braiders made their rugs different and original.

10

DESIGN IN BRAIDED RUGS

Design in braided rugs comes from the way we put our colors against each other not only in strands but in the arrangement of the rows The results of juxtaposition show a wide variety of individual tastes. We have quietly blended harmonious rugs which give us a feeling of rest and tranquillity; we have bright contrasting colors which give us gaiety and liveliness; we have bold geometric patterns spread all over the rug with strongly contrasting colors; we have tailored-looking rugs with the little patterns used with only a few well-chosen colors; and we have the old-time, cheery "HIT-OR-MISS" rugs with every color used in profusion and sprinkled all over with black. We have set patterns using bands of many colors for several rows and between them a solid row of an outstanding color, generally the darkest color used in your rug or perhaps certain colors which the braider wishes to emphasize.

In addition to the regulation round or oval rugs, we have the rectangular-shaped ones now becoming very popular, and all the fancy shapes which women with a desire for originality can create. Some of our rugs are definitely streamlined; others are still a hodge-podge, made up of what is in the rag bag, just something to cover the floor as in the Colonial days.

The old "HIT-OR-MISS" rug of long ago days was decidedly the result of necessity for a floor covering. Some latent artistic ability was shown by the arrangement of the colors with the concentric rounds of the solid black setting off these gay divisions. That first design is still used widely, but the trend is unmistakably for rugs which fit the *décor* of the braider's home.

Our world is made up of straight lines and curves. As we examine a braid, we find that the contour is a gentle curve along the edges. Yet, as the strands are braided together, angles or echelons are formed down through the center of the braid. When braids are laced together, triangles or arrowheads are formed and we coil these strands of braid into round mats. Even our square-cornered rugs have slight curves to the corners.

Too many round or oval rugs curl up and many a round center becomes shaped like a Mexican hat. Start with your bends made in the braid, and then, with your three and three increases, you need never worry about either a round rug nor will you have the experience which I had with my first oval.

This was to have been a complete surprise for my mother who made many braided rugs. I had been married but a few years and was always trying out new crafts just as she did. This mat did not grow too large. Instead it surprised me as well as my mother by curling up on all the edges from lack of enough increases. Our Airedale puppy loved it for it provided cozy sleeping quarters for him. I was reminded of my first attempt at braiding at an exhibition where I had some footstool covers minus the footstools for which they had been made. They were lying upside down on a table, and much to my amusement, they were picked up and worked over as many of the spectators tried to flatten them out, confiding the while that they could sympathize with me for that was just what had happened to their rugs. What was I going to do to flatten them out? As it happened, an oval cover *was* almost flattened out by the pulling of well-wishers who practically ruined it before I realized what was going on and rescued it.

When you have learned simple braiding, lacing, increasing, and turning a modified or sharp square corner, you will be ready to make all the so called "fancy" rugs you like and in the very simplest fashion. Even the multiple strands will hold no problems for you, and with a distinct color guide to follow, you can have a rug made of subtly blending colors or a handsome, distinctive one with many patterns.

Whether you turn in raw edges with your fingers or with the metal cones makes no difference, as long as they are turned in all the way to the middle of the fold, and whether you have the open folds to the left or the right will not matter if they are well turned in. Just remember that if they are at the left, the open folds will be on the outside of the rug. However, if it is easier for you, put them on your left, and on the last butted row, you can put them inside.

In 1953 when I showed some of my unusual rugs on television on the "How Show," sponsored by the Massachusetts State Department of Vocational Training for Adults, I was besieged by inquiries from all over New England. Braiders wanted more detail on how I turned square corners and on how I put in the little designs. Massachusetts and New Hampshire women were especially alert to new ideas, and through the Department I sent out hundreds of copies of a free pamphlet. A year later, I published *Let's Braid a Rug* which has been sold in every state and in three foreign countries. There is a tremendous satisfaction in knowing that so many women are working to improve their homespun crafts and to make a real art of their braiding.

As far as the small designs go, there is nothing new about them. They were used centuries ago by the rug weavers of Asia in making their lovely oriental rugs, and they are still being used today. The Navaho Indians also use these same little geometric patterns in their blankets.

Years ago, when women sewed their braids together, many of them put in the designs by fulling in the materials when going around a curve, so that the designs would appear on the second side of an oval as well as on the first. In *The Craft of Hand-Made Rugs* by Amy Hicks, published in 1920, a few pages are devoted to braided rugs made of cotton. The author explains too how the arrowhead was formed.

There may be many women in various parts of the country who have discovered little designs for themselves and use them. It is always interesting to find how they try colors against each other in strands to find what adjacent colors will give new effects. If the colors are in contrast, the designs may be more quickly detected. As long as you adhere to the rule of three increases to the shoulder of a curve or six to an end of an oval, the patterns will be clear on the ends and sides of an oval rug. The nearer to each other the three increases are put, the sooner will the design reappear.

Today, braiders are very pattern-conscious. They plan their successive rows to keep a design, going from one to another in succession. The more one does of them, the more intriguing they become. Even though none of the small designs may be very noticeable in the body of the rug, most women like the arrowhead to finish off the last two rows. This pattern seems to give a finished appearance to almost any rug, and is heavy enough to hold the rug to the floor if the darker shades are used. Many of the rugs shown have this arrowhead border.

arrowhead

The simplest of the ancient designs consisted of two straight lines put together at an angle to form an arrowhead. When we use three different colors in a braid, such as gray, green and red, and follow

arrow

row 1

row 2

FIGURE 17

this row with one in which we drop the green and use two reds and a gray, we have the potential for the arrowhead design. But when we are lacing, we must place the two reds against the one red of the previous row so that they will be on either side of it. Thus we give the triangular shape to the red color loops and we have our arrowhead. Note that this is done with only two rows.

ric-rac

For this design, make the first two rows as for an arrowhead. In the third row, use one red and any two other contrasting colors.

ric-rac

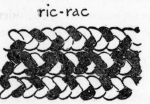

FIGURE 18

Place this one red between the two reds of the previous row. Note that this pattern takes three rows to complete. (See "COUNTRY KITCHEN.")

diamond

The diamond is really two arrowheads with rows 2 and 3, which are alike, put against each other as you lace. The reds in the four rows run 1,2,2,1. In other words, the diamond is the arrowhead in reverse.

diamond

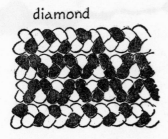

FIGURE 19

double diamonds or diagonals

Double diamonds are a continuation of the single diamonds, with one gray and two reds in each row, with the same colors kept against each other when lacing. Even if the grays are not all the same, if the color values are of equal intensity the diagonal design will still be apparent. Many centers are worked out this way and even entire rugs. Much of "TRANQUILLITY" and "OCTOBER HILLS" are wide bands of shaded color showing unobtrusive diagonals.

jewels

For jewels, we separate strong colors so that they never come in juxtaposition with each other, appearing as "dots" scattered over the surface. Colors like strong gold, bright blue, brilliant red or vivid green are all better separated. In this way, their intensity is distributed and they look like rich jewels scattered over your rug. Remember that in the ancient court rugs of Asian potentates, they put real jewels in their rugs. We can have our favorite yet practical and inexpensive jewels in the rugs we make today. "PATCHWORK" has lovely green "emeralds" and "BETSY ROSS" has red rubies and blue sapphires. Imagination? Oh well, how could we live without it? It adds lots of spice to our rugs when we work on them alone, and we can become the richest people in the world. So use yours and make a rich rug of jewels!

butterflies

When two loops come at an angle in adjacent rows and are kept that way against contrasting colors, we call them "butterflies." These may often be the centers of diamonds but because they stand out more than the diamonds, we give them this name. Such are the apricot and peach butterflies of "SILVER GLINTS" and the yellow and gold butterflies of "GOLDEN LATTICE."

chain stitch

This is produced by a row of solid color such as navy or black. For the next two rows, use three different colors which contrast well against each other and against the solid band, such as rose, green and a light beige tweed. Keep the same colors against each other as you lace, and make your fourth row of the same solid color as Row 1. (See "BLOCK AND ROSETTE" border.)

flower design

Between two rows of greens, use two rows made up of 1 soft green and 2 pink. Keep the pinks together as you lace, so you will have the effect of a pink blossom with a pale green center. The solid rows of greens on either side may be darker than the green used with the pink petals. Medium blues with gold can be used between blue greens, reds with green, etc. (See "APPLE BLOSSOM TIME.")

lacy edge

For a lacy look to your rug, use two light colors or tweeds with one dark or contrasting color, followed by a row of the solid color. Your dark color seems to melt away from the edge of the previous row, and gives you a lacy effect. It this is used several times in a rug, the overall effect will be very airy and graceful. Sometimes it just "happens," but if you plan for it, so much the better. (See "MERRY-GO-ROUND.")

geometric patterns

For a real block or geometric design, use the multiple strand braid with from 5-7-9 strands, and try putting various colors against each other to work out an individual design. Use two or more pairs, if you wish, of the same colors or tweed mixtures, keeping them together side by side on your large safety pin. (See "BLOCK AND ROSETTE" and "CHECKERBOARD.")

lacing patterned rugs

For those who butt, there is no problem of keeping the same colors against each other in each row, for we are careful to put them in place as we start a new round. The continuous braiders may, occasionally, have to increase an extra loop when they join a new color to keep their designs.

A word of warning when you are making several rows alike or with one or two of the same colors, should be given to those who are butting each row. See that each color goes on the safety pin in the same position as the previous row—in the 1, 2, or 3 place or your pattern will be thrown off.

For those who are making rugs for modern homes, these small pattern designs can be very striking. For those who want just a good rug, they can add interest to an accumulation of tweeds and mixtures, and a few colors used judiciously with such designs can add sparkle to the whole rug. For those who want blended harmonious shades, pattern can be introduced into the background to give a textured feeling to the plain colors. They will add unity and their repetition will bring balance into the entire rug.

11

DARE TO BE DIFFERENT—
UNUSUAL RUGS

Many braiders make unusual rugs as far as their colors and patterns go, while others are constantly working out different shapes for their mats. Through the years and in many states, I have seen a variety of these and some have become very popular.

The round rug, for instance, has been doubled to form wheels and is often found in Massachusetts. I have always felt that such a rug was out of balance and have never encouraged its making in my groups. I do approve the "three circle" rug, patterned after the old one found in New Hampshire years ago with varying sizes as to the centers. Such a rug is "MERRY-GO-ROUND," starting with three 26-in. circles. "CONTENTMENT" is a lovely 6 x 9 rug started with three 12-in. circles, and was the first braided rug Mrs. Billington ever made.

While there used to be a lot of butting to these rugs, we now make the sharp square corners (on the right of the braid) at each indentation and pull up the center loop with our pliers so that it fits into the point between the two circles. As the rug grows larger, these spaces grow wider and we use the modified square corner, always on the right of the braid, to fill the gaps. After several rows, we can make a straight braid.

A "clover leaf" type rug like "BOUQUET OF ZINNIAS," is treated in the same way for these spaces between the circles as are the spaces in the rug called "GOLDEN GLOW." In "BOUQUET OF ZINNIAS," the center has been filled with small butted pieces. In "GOLDEN GLOW," the center has a double-hooked triangular piece with my initials and date on one side while the other side is simply hooked with two shades of the outer edge of the circles. The double hooking makes the rug absolutely reversible. This shows what one can do to a large hooked center to eliminate any appearance of tape on the wrong side of the hooked section.

I have seen many attempts to make rugs of from five to thirteen circles but have yet to see one which was color-appealing enough with the centers neatly filled. Sometimes these were left open, "for the dirt to fall through" as one woman described it.

Lots of short ends can be used up in circles in a hit-or-miss fashion, with the accent colors which you want to predominate making up the braids which surround the centers. If you want an all-over pattern in a 9 x 12 oval rug, you can start it with three circles, each 12 inches in diameter. As the rug grows, the scallops diminish and by the time it is 9 x 12, you will have your oval rug.

Rugs like "SCALLOPED ROSE" and "STARLIGHT" also start with round centers. Next, a row is attached which goes out in arms or in points, evenly spaced around the center. These rugs can be made any size according to the diameter of the circle with which you start, and the length and shape of the "arms" pushed out. This point must be decided as soon as the center is the desired size. By using modified square corners, we can round the ends of the arms gently, or we can use the sharp square corners as for the points in a star.

One of my pupils who lives in a house built in 1774, made a rug like "STARLIGHT" which measures 9 ft. across. She uses this under an old square rosewood piano and is filling her lovely old home with beautifully made unusual braided rugs. Another braider copied "STARLIGHT" in shades of yellow, green and brown. The others in that class soon gave her rug another name—they called it "Brown-Eyed Susan." It was most appropriate and proved to be a prize-winning rug.

Five points are used in "STARLIGHT" because of the stars in our flag. Five, six or seven gently rounded would be better if you want your rug to look like a flower. Choose suitable shades of colors for these rugs.

Numerous square hallways call for mats the same shape, and these are made like all square-cornered rugs. For these, my choice of corners is made with the sharp method, for the rug can start immediately with four corners like "DOMINO."

A long hall-runner may be made like the "GLAD WELCOME" or like any rectangular rug, squaring with the first two braids.

A stair-runner like "MEMORY LANE" is made in straight strips, bound off and surrounded by a few butted rows to form a border. "MEMORY LANE" had to go around four stairs, turning sharp angles. The photographer tried to show the curve in the stairs at the top but it was quite impossible. After making a 30-ft. straight runner, I had to cut pie-shaped wedges from the braids to make the turns and then butt the ends carefully together. I could never have done a neat joining in such cramped quarters if I had not used the Number 7 method of butting.

When making a straight stair-runner, measure the tread and the riser and allow 1½ inches more for each step. A braided runner will take up that much more as it goes over the tread. A stair-runner is heavy and is reversible if one straight piece. It should be put down firmly with strong tacks and rods like "MEMORY LANE," with rubber rug-lining underneath the treads. This will prevent any chance of accident.

Stair-treads may be ovals or rectangles, or they can be straight pieces for a turn in the stairs, with bound edges and the last row butted on for a border. The only thing needed to hold these treads in position is a strip of rubber rug-lining which you can buy by the yard and cut into shape. This rubber lining, particularly the thicker type, is what I advise using under hooked centers which have braided borders and for any small mats not large enough or heavy enough to hold fast to the floor. This will prevent accidents when there are lots of little feet running through a house.

A diagonal weave effect can be used effectively throughout an entire rug. Start by keeping the same colors against each other when lacing. Use two like colors if possible, with a contrasting color to set the pattern. The rug can be kept in these same colors throughout, as is explained in the chapter on design. Or you can have a monochromatic rug, blending out into various shades of one color or tweeds to give that effect. Such a rug as the latter is "GOLDEN LATTICE" which blends from yellows and tans to golden browns, with rust and brown tweedy mixtures adding to the lively look of the overall appearance of the whole rug.

Instead of making a square or rectangular rug, you may use six or eight sides to give your rug individuality. Start these as for a circle and mark off as soon as the diameter is large enough for the number of sides you wish. Square in the braid as you lace.

"MINE ALONE" shows how you can establish claim to your own work. The center was originally made for a chair-seat. Then I decided to braid in my initials and the date. Sharp corners are necessary for letters with right angles, while for a gentle curve, the modified square corners are more suitable.

This little mat may give you an idea of how to make a round rug with a center of earth brown surrounded by soft greens, but instead of the letters, put in some red roses, perhaps six of them, made with modified square corners to round them. Place these at even intervals around your circle, attaching at the base with a few stitches to hold in position. Put your outside rows of green at the top and attach to hold the tops of the roses in place. Now fill the spaces between the roses with butted braids of shaded greens. Make enclosed ends on both ends of the butted pieces and sew into place.

Have you ever braided a cover for a footstool? They are very simple to make. If your stool is round, proceed as for a round mat until the top is covered. Taper gently if you have been making a continuous braid. The next two or three braids will be butted and will be laced very tight from the right side without any increasing. This pulls in the circumference of the circle, acting like a drawstring. Two braids are usually enough to make the top fit real snug.

If your stool is oval, measure length and width, subtract the difference and start with that length for a center as for an oval rug. Make it continuous or butted. If continuous, taper gently when the top can be covered with the mat. Now turn to the right side and butt two or three rows without increases to pull in the sides. You can pull in the mat more and fit the cover more tightly by working on the right side. Hold it in your hands while you work.

If your stool is rectangular, square your corners either in the braid or as you lace, according to the sharpness of the wood, and proceed as for the other types of stool-covers.

braided bags

Have you ever wanted to make a braided bag? You can use two circles or an oval, depending upon your own taste. Attach around the ends or sides according to whether it is a round bag or one made with an oval. Leave enough for a comfortable opening. You can leave the last braid or two loose for a handle, or you can make them separate and attach firmly. Both ways are acceptable. I have had the bags lined in plastic, cretonne or plain cambric lining. You can make them of printed cottons too. Tear strips 3 inches wide.

sandals

I have seen, though have never made, sandals of braids, made in narrow ovals, with cross pieces of braids over the toes to hold them on the feet.

toy animals

A pussy cat may be made large enough for a mat to be used in a child's room or it may be made for something to cuddle at night when the child goes to bed. I have a grandson who, at four, still likes his cat to lie beside him when he goes to sleep. These cats are very lovable and easy to make.

Try to find soft fleecy woolens in white, beige, gray or gray mixtures, tan mixtures, black. These colors will braid up to look like the bodies of real cats.

For the little one, make a circle about 8 inches in diameter for the head. Taper it off carefully. The next row around, point up two ears with sharp square corners, leaving an opening like a V upside down. These openings will be filled with soft pink woolen cloth or with pink felt. Now make a circle about 14 inches in diameter, but do not taper the end. We need about 10 inches loose for the tail. Enclose the end as when butting, and catch up half way on the circle with a few strong stitches. Sew the two circles together at the neck line, making sure the ears are in the right position.

Use shiny green buttons for eyes, sewn onto elliptical-shaped pieces of tan wool, a triangular piece of red wool for the nostrils, and another piece for the tongue. The tongues and eyes can do much to give cute expressions to the cats. For whiskers, use pipe cleaners drawn through the loops on either side of the mouth. Use a pencil to darken the pipe cleaners a trifle. If you want something softer than pipe cleaners, use soft yarn and stitch into position.

For a bunny, use soft fleecy white, beige or gray material. Make an oval about 8 x 13 inches for the body, and another about 4 x 5 for the head, this to be attached on a slant. Make two 4-inch-long ears, made pointed by sharp square corners. Line these ears, as for the cat, with pink woolen cloth. The feet should be short, not over two inches long and two braids wide, to look like two pairs of feet set close together, and these should be put under the body on a slant towards the left to make the rabbit look as if he were squatting. The tail should set high at the end of his back, about 1½ inches long. Mrs. Ruth Hogarth of Wrentham, Massachusetts, adds an extra fillip to Mr. Cottontail by lining the stubby tail with a bit of white cotton. Whiskers of pipe cleaners or white yarn, pink-button glass eyes over a beige eyeball, and a real pink ribbon around his neck complete a soft toy which will appeal to the younger fry. All the cats wear real red ribbons tied around their necks, and one might add a little bell.

One woman who had never before seen these little braided toys was so impressed that she told me she was going home to make a braided lamb for her little granddaughter's room, one large enough to walk on.

A Mrs. Elizabeth Greaney of Manchester, Connecticut, made a prize-winning cat large enough to be used as a mat. Instead of the regulation tan and yellow and white ordinary calico cats, she made hers of the hit-or-miss type, and used all colors with black. She has also made a turtle rug for a child's room. The center started with a small fat oval, was given five "arms" which were dark in color to represent the turtle. It was surrounded with lighter colors, so that it was outlined and looked like a real turtle.

braided borders
for hooked rugs

As all of us who make hooked rugs know, edges which are not reinforced in some way become frayed and worn long before the rest of the rug shows any wear. This is especially true of those rugs which are not made with a double thickness of burlap through which the last few rows are hooked. In mid-Victorian days, hookers often put a protective border of braids around their centers. Today that fashion has reached a high peak.

There are a number of points to remember when we do this. If we decide to use a braided border before we start the hooking, we can lay the foundation for a flat-lying rug if the tape is first shrunk by soaking it in hot water so that when it is sewn to the burlap, it will not pull later when the finished rug is pressed.

To attach the tape, lay it inside the pattern with the edge against the black line, marking the outside of the rug. With the tape towards you as you sew, baste it on, being careful that you do not pull the tape taut. After it is basted, sew on the machine. Turn it back and pin to the burlap, so it will be out of the way while you hook the design.

When the hooking is finished and the burlap is removed from your frame, cut the burlap almost to the width of the tape and baste it back to the wrong side of the rug. Now baste back the tape, first near the edge of the rug, then at the edge of the tape against the burlap. Now sew it down firmly with an over-and-over stitch.

To enhance the beauty of your center instead of detracting from it, use a braided border not any wider than from ⅛ to ½ of the width of your hooked center, making small braids to conform to the fineness of your hooking. Do not try to put in any little designs which might vie for interest, remembering that the border is simply a frame for your hooked mat. It is better to avoid trying to use all the colors you used in hooking. Use only the predominating ones to "spread out" the rug and make you feel that there is no break between the hooking and the braiding.

Start your first rows with the background colors of the hooking, and blend harmoniously into the deeper shades. It is a simple rule but a good one to have each row pick up at least one color from the preceding row. This is a rule we follow in braiding monochromatic rugs or in rainbow-like rugs.

The first braid is sewn to the tape with a strong thread such as "Aunt Lydia's," while all others are interlocked closely together.

Victorian Elegance

Each row is butted, with the joinings coming at different places around the rug.

It makes no difference what the shape of your hooked rug may be, for you can turn sharp or modified square corners for rectangular rugs and the inverted square corners for scalloped or indented ovals or scalloped circles. All of the various kinds have been done successfully in my classes.

If your rug seems thinner in the center than in the braided border, use the sponge-rubber lining for the center to equalize the thickness. If you plan before you start a rug, you can hook high and make small, narrow braids.

If your center is an especially "busy" one or something you want to be outstanding, enlarge it by one color only—your background color —and starting with the weakest value, work out to the deepest shades. Dyed tweeds will often give a fine lively yet subdued appearance to these borders where the heavier and closely woven suedes and fleeces tend to give a solid, heavy or even ponderous look to the whole rug.

If the hooked background covers a large area, it might be more effective to use many different colors in the border, tied together with tweeds of the same background.

multiple strand rugs

Multiple strands may be used to make small mats or, as in Colonial days, they may be the answer to the need for a large carpet. Many braiders of today think that these rugs are something new and difficult to make and they are agreeably surprised to find that they have been made for generations and that they braid up very fast.

An old Englishman said he learned as a boy to braid with a rack which had hooks on it. He made braids with as many as eleven strands in them. Today our boys are learning this multiple-strand braiding when they make belts in their manual training classes.

If, instead of using any pieces which come to hand, you try out some contrasting colors, with tweeds if you wish, you may be able to work out some very interesting geometric patterns to be carried throughout the entire rug. I saw a handsome rug made with seven strands with umbered shades of blue-greens.

It is best to use odd numbers like 3, 5, 7, 9. Odd numbers can be interlaced while the even numbers must be sewn together in strips.

I used to make tubes of my multiple strands by basting them so that I would be sure no raw edges were left in sight and so that I could braid fast. Today I slip on the braid-aids and forget the tubing and I braid these multiple strand braids much faster than I once did. It would be best for the novice to confine her efforts to a five-strand braid. Choose the strands carefully and if you have two alike, put them side by side to give a block effect. If you don't like the resultant braid, try the colors in a different position, but do keep those same colors together.

If you make straight strips as in "BLOCK AND ROSETTE," you must change the order of the colors on your safety pin—a large-size safety pin takes care of five or six strands very nicely—by moving the one on the farthest left to the farthest right with each braid that you make. If you forget to do this, you will waste cloth when you put them together and try to match the colors against each other. Each color moves once to the left with each row.

In multiple strands, the strand at your farthest left is worked over to the right, by plaiting or weaving it—call it what you wish—over and under in turn until it is on the right. Then the outer strand on the left goes through the same process, and so it goes—moving over and under to the right. Do it slowly at first to see what is happening to your strands. After a while you will see that you are braiding with both hands. The process really consists of putting the strands at your left over and under while you braid three strands with your right hand.

The strands at the right work gradually toward the left and then back to the right again, each in turn. If you inadvertently skip one of the turns, all your pattern will be thrown off, so check the orders of colors on the side very frequently at first, to make sure that each strand is in order.

You can use enclosed ends to start each row and finish in the same way, with a few butted rows around the whole rug. Or you can sew across the top and bottom to hold straight, bind, and call it finished. Or as I like to do, make a few three-strand braids as a border.

These rugs work up fast with five strands, but more than five require special equipment to braid on. I presume one could make a board with hooks on it, or look for an extra-size safety pin like the old horse-blanket pins. Do not start one of these rugs unless you are proficient at three-strand braiding. It is like making argyle socks with many things dangling into your lap at once. The strands should be kept rolled up so they can be disentangled easily. If you want to make such a rug, try a small one first, to become accustomed to manipulating a handful of strands at once.

The geometric patterns are most intriguing, but you must have enough of each material so that you can keep the same pattern throughout the rug.

One of my pupils tells me that she is going to make a five-strand braid for a wall-to-wall carpet for her large living room. She will use 1 black strand throughout, 2 strands of tweed mixtures, whatever comes to hand, while the fourth and fifth ones are to be made up of any bright colors she can lay her hands on at the moment. It sounds wonderful, and I am looking forward to seeing it.

When you have enough strips braided to give you the desired width for your rug, sew across the top firmly, by hand or sewing machine, making sure that you keep the same width for each strip. Bind with a 1¼ in.-wide strip of whatever color you will use in the next row of three-strand braid which you are going to use as a border. Turn the binding to the wrong side and stitch down carefully with blind stitches.

You can use a border of one shaded color, or as in "BLOCK AND ROSETTE," pick up three outstanding colors and keeping the same colors against each other to form a chainlike pattern, make two or three rows of this braid.

You can make a rectangular rug of multiple strands, in the same way that you square three-strand braid. Put 1 over 2, 2 over 1, 1 over 2 and hold on to that Strand 2 braid with the left hand while you braid the others under and over. You are really braiding with your right hand. When you have Strand 3 over in 2's place, make your three turns from the left as before and hang on to Strand 3 while you braid the others from the right. This completes the square corner for the five-strand braid and the order of colors on the side works out as in the original. Remember it takes the "three and three" turns repeated for this multiple strand to square itself. You may have a little difficulty in braiding the four strands in your right hand, but the left hand also works, and after you have done it a few times, it becomes a simple knack.

For an oval rug with multiple strands, if you will pull hard on the right-hand strands, your rug will curve naturally.

The above directions are for those who start their multiple strands from the left. I number them from left to right, as 1, 2, 3, 4, 5. The squaring process would be the same whether you start from the left or the right.

pillows

Make your pillows of wool or of velvet, of silks or of cotton prints, or make them of velour or of upholstery fabrics. Make the round ones, the oval-shaped or square—just like two tops for footstools—and lace together, leaving a large enough opening for the pillow, insert and finish lacing.

12
WITCHES' BREW—
ART OF DYEING

"Double, double toil and trouble;
  Fire burn, and cauldron bubble."

The above lines of the witches in Shakespeare's *Macbeth* might well come to mind if we had to dye our cloth in the long tedious way it was done a hundred years ago. Tramping through fields and woods to find berries, madder, sassafras, butternuts, birch bark and so many of the plants which had to be boiled down in the big dye kettles was a real chore for the women in those days. When cochineal was used for the reds and indigo for the blues, these could be bought at the general stores in the villages.

Before World War I our good dye stuffs came from Germany but in the period since that time, dyes have undergone radical changes. Today we have excellent dyes that do not bleed; they are fast and true to color and are distributed in a wide variety of shades.

Diamond Dyes used to be standard dyes for those of us here in New England years ago. Cushing's Perfection Dyes and Putnam Dyes now seem to be the ones most used, with the wide variety of the Perfection Dyes much liked by hookers and braiders as well. They are both powder dyes and must be dissolved and cooked by boiling. Both are highly satisfactory.

The Perfection Dyes come in such an expansive range of beautiful shades and colors that after one experience with them, you will always want to use them. Both of these companies also have a bleach powder to remove the original color of the goods before you dye it. Cushing also puts out Larvasol, a powder which, put into the dye bath, moth-proofs as it dyes.

The directions on packages are for dyeing over white. As few of us are able to obtain all the white we need for our dyeing, we dye over beige, light gray and mixtures of these colors, and we must take into consideration the effect these colors will have on our results. Any light mixture which has a preponderance of light grays and beiges can be used to give us softer and grayer tones in our colors, perhaps just what is needed in our rugs instead of the sharper color we would achieve if we dyed over white. When we dye, we rarely use a whole package which contains enough to do a whole pound of white.

All light shades of cloth can be deepened, but if only dark colors are on hand and you need some light shades, you should use the color remover first before you attempt to dye. If you have no color remover, try cooking the fabric in Lux Flakes with a teaspoon of ammonia added to two quarts of water. Too much ammonia will rot your cloth, so use care.

Some materials are much more difficult to dye than others because they have been chemically treated to make them crease-resistant Plurasol, put out by Cushing's Perfection Dyes, will soften the fibers and make them fit for dyeing. Hard-finished materials and those closely woven should be soaked well in very warm water, so that they are thoroughly wet. It takes much longer for these woolens to absorb moisture than loosely woven goods. If they are put into your dye pot wet only on the surface, you will have a spotty dyed cloth.

It is fun to experiment with middle grays and tans. A middle-value gray dyed with jade was one of the loveliest soft greens I have ever seen.

Don't discard good cloth because it is faded. That is where your little package of dye performs miracles. The new colors come out fresh yet soft and are a delight to use.

If you have pink and don't want to strip it, dye over it with deeper shades of its own color or with rose, strawberry, cherry, wine, garnet or maroon. If it is on the yellow side, try crimson, terra cotta, Egyptian red. Mahogany ties in exceptionally well with old rose shades. Mulberry over a bluish pink gives a beautiful rich tone; and all the rust and brown shades can be obtained from the pinks.

If you have lots of pale blue, use yellow or gold over it for a pretty green or use myrtle or dark green; use turquoise or peacock for a handsome blue or use old gold for a bronze tone. If you have a strong blue which may be too intense to put on the floor, gray it with a speck of orange, its complementary color, or with a thin dye of silver-gray.

You can gray any strong color with a weak dye of its complement, but be sure it *is* a weak dye as too strong a solution would make a color resembling mud.

Light gray and gray mixtures take readily to reseda, myrtle or turquoise greens, while the beige and beige mixtures are excellent for gold, old gold, hunter green, bronze and olive greens, and all the yellow-brown family, including the tans, golden and mummy brown and the rusts, and the wood rose, terra cotta and deep browns.

If you are dyeing over white and do not want too much intensity of color, a bit of silver-gray added to the dye solution will act as if you were dyeing over light gray and soften the color.

Black may be dyed over any color. Over red, it may come out a rusty or antique shade, but if you add a little green dye to the solution, you will have a better or purer black. If you are dyeing over blue, a truer black will result if you add a little orange to the dye pot.

If you use bright green over a gray and black mixture, you will have a very acceptable green tweed.

Add a speck of bright green to your bronze-green dye over beige mixture for a lively yet soft yellow green.

Add a speck of dark green to your cardinal or garnet for bright reds. You will find that just a speck of its complement will enrich a color to a far more acceptable shade.

If you find some threads are different colors from the rest of the cloth after the dyeing process is finished, the chances are that they are not wool but one of the new synthetics such as rayon, dacron, nylon. Cushing's Perfection All-Purpose Dyes should be used over the material if you think that it is not all wool.

Loosely woven materials such as tweedy mixtures absorb the dye readily and boiling will thicken what might be too thin a fabric for a rug. Thick, closely woven suedes take more time to dye. As in the soaking process, they absorb moisture slowly and you may have to cook them as much as fifteen minutes more than a batch of tweedy or more loosely woven woolens for the same depth of color.

Flannels dye well, but use only the heavier ones. The thin ones such as those used for women's dresses, will not wear so well under foot. If you feel you must use them, cut the strips wide and crush them into a thick strand or line them with the same color. Any thin material picks up dye quickly.

You will find it easier to dye woolens which are thick if they are torn into strips, always making sure that you leave almost one eighth inch wider than what you need, to allow for shrinkage.

Let's see what is needed for our dyeing:

1   Dyes to be fast, must be boiled or simmered gently. Do not think that you can dye your woolens by twirling them for a few minutes in the washing machine. You can tint them or color them, but they will not retain their color very long.

2   Use a dye kettle or a white enamel dishpan or even, if you haven't a large vessel, an ordinary white washbasin will suffice. You don't need to do a great quantity at a time. A washbasin will take a half yard, and it is easier if you tear it in strips up to a quarter or a third of a yard in length. Never have more in your basin than can be completely immersed in the dye bath without crowding. About two quarts of water in a washbasin will dye a half yard of tweedy materials very comfortably.

3   Be sure your fabric is clean and have it thoroughly soaked in

warm water. While it is soaking, prepare the dye solution and have the hot water simmering on your stove.

4   Solution: Put a teaspoonful of dye into a cup with enough warm water to make a paste—a tablespoonful is enough. Fill the cup with boiling water and mix thoroughly. (There are about 24 teaspoonfuls to a cup.)

If you are dyeing for four shades, you can add 3 teaspoonfuls of your dye solution to the water for the first or weakest shade, then 5 teaspoonfuls for the 2nd shade, 7 for the third shade, and 9 for the deepest or 4th shade.

For three shades, you may like to add 4, 8 or 12 teaspoonfuls to your water in turn for less gradation and a bit more contrast with deeper shades.

Remember it takes less dye for materials which may have a little of the shade you wish already in them, such as a pink which you may be changing to a rust, or a beige and brown tweed which you may be overdyeing with gold. Use your dye sparingly over anything but white.

Put your first solution into the water in the basin and let dissolve thoroughly. I use two smooth, strong, flat sticks like those used by house painters to mix their paints. These are excellent for stirring and lifting the cloth.

Wring out your soaked material gently and add to the simmering dye bath. If put into the basin when the water is boiling hard, the pieces first in may absorb more dye than the rest of the strips. Bring to a boil and boil *gently* until the dye is all taken up or until the cloth is the desired color, remembering that wet cloth is always much darker than dry cloth. Stir constantly. Remove from the water and place in another container nearby. About 10 minutes are enough cooking time.

Repeat the process with the next shade, adding enough water to replace any taken up by the first batch. (I let the first batch drip over the basin to allow as much excess water as possible to stay in the dye bath. The two sticks will hold it above the pan.) If some dye is still in the water, make allowance for it when you add your next solution.

In turn, dye your three or four shades. You may not use all your dye solution, but you can save any left over for your next batch. Put it into a small covered jar such as baby foods come in and mark for future use.

When your shades are all dyed, add more water to the dye bath, and put in a tablespoonful of non-iodized salt. Now add the first batch and boil gently for about 15 minutes. The dye bath is now probably clear and your color is all set.

Remove cloth, and put into a basin of warm clear water.

Do this with each batch, adding more salt and more water as needed, and rinse in clear warm water until all materials are free of excess dye and the water is clear. Squeeze gently and hang to dry, preferably in the wind or outside where the wrinkles will blow free. Do not press if you can help it.

You will find that dark colors take a little longer to dye than the lighter shades. I have cooked some for as long as a half hour when the material was closely woven.

By letting your cloth set after it is removed from the dye bath after the first boiling, it will absorb the dye thoroughly and the salt immersion will take less time.

Some people like to dye their darkest values first, and then what is left in turn. These will be the lighter shades. Either way is satisfactory and as you do more dyeing, you will find certain shortcuts which are easier for you than the above methods. One woman uses a very large dye kettle, doing a yard at a time and does all her rinsing in her washing machine. I do mine in the sink. If I don't have the strips torn before soaking, I tear them while they are still wet and avoid the lint which always appears when the strips are torn off dry cloth.

Do not use cold water for rinsing as it hardens the fibers of your cloth and makes them stiff.

Strips are easier to handle in the dye bath than wide pieces and will give you more evenly dyed cloth.

When dye comes off on your hands as you braid, you have not rinsed out the excess dye. You may need two or three rinses if you have used too much dye in the bath.

One teaspoon of dye may do as much as a yard of material which is a mixture of an off-white. Each package of dye will do a pound of white material in the strong intensity of the hue. There are about two teaspoons of dye in each package.

As soon as you have dyed, label your work, so you will know

what you used to gain such an effect. Cut off a little piece of a dyed strip and let it dry against its original strip. Keep these two pieces together, labeled in a notebook. They will prove invaluable to you when you wish to duplicate the shade later.

Have bits of the original cloth and bits of the dyed shades side by side in your notebook and under them the formula you used for each shade. These notebooks should be like the recipes for your favorite desserts—easy to get at and easy to follow and to exchange with your fellow braiders.

If woolens do not respond to the same dyeing, do not blame the wools. Wools from different sheep take different colors and chemicals put into water affect our dyeing, as do the chemicals put with woolens to make them wrinkle-proof.

If you add salt to the dye bath immediately, your dye will be taken up so fast that the color will be uneven. This may work out when you are dyeing a small piece in a large basin where the whole thing can be immersed at once, but if you are striving for clear colors, it is better to dye first in clear water without the salt and add it later to set the color.

The above directions are for simple dyeing. If, when your colors have dried, they are too light, you can re-dye them with a stronger solution in your dye bath. If they are too deep, you will have the job of removing some of the color. It is far easier to dye lighter than too dark, but better still, dye just right. If you keep that record of your experiments, you will not repeat mistakes.

Sometimes we have deliberately splotched effects in our dyeing. We call this "spot-dyeing." In "AUTUMN WINDS," which has a hooked center of autumn leaves, I spot-dyed for the leaves and for part of the border, in order to carry out the idea of the vari-colored leaves strewn around the braided border.

For this type of dyeing, we do not use the dye solution. We use the plain powdered dye with salt. For the autumn border, three different red dyes and five green were used over a pale yellow. The strips to be dyed were torn 3⅛ inches wide and were well soaked in warm water and wrung dry.

Into a pan holding a cup of hot water, I laid about 6 inches of a strip with the end outside the pan to keep it from the dye. That part in the pan was sprinkled with a little chartreuse dye and over it, a little salt. The cloth was folded over and the next few inches were sprinkled with dry aqua green and then the salt. The cloth was folded again and the next few inches sprinkled with dry bronze green, salt; turned over and in turn sprinkled with crimson and salt, olive green and salt, turkey red and salt, plain green dye and salt, cardinal and salt. Between each of the dye sprinklings, a little of the original yellow piece of cloth, free from dye, was left.

When all of the cloth had been used this way, crowded and packed into the pan, a cover was put on the basin and the heat turned on to simmer intensity. When you are doing this spot-dyeing, make sure that the cover is tight so the cloth will steam, and never have the heat above the simmering stage or the water will evaporate and the cloth will be scorched. Simmer for ten minutes.

Take the pan off the stove, and let set for another ten minutes. Rinse in tepid water until the colors do not run. You will have a very variegated strip of cloth which will braid like plaids. If you want to make a rug for a boy's room and cannot find plaids, make your own varied strips this way over any light base and using colors which you need to have outstanding.

Years ago it was the fad to buy a yard of thin pale-colored silk for a scarf, tie it into knots, and dye it. This method of dyeing is still used for variegated shades of the same color, for when it is taken from the dye bath, untied and dried, there will be a multi-shaded piece of cloth.

The simple method described first is the one we use most. If we want to add a speck of color to deepen our shades, we can add green to the red dyes, orange to the blues, bright green to bronze green, black to crimson and so on. Experimenting with your dyes will teach you much about combinations of colors. This is where your color wheel will be studied. The complements used for strengthening are acquired by the addition of a mere speck of dye. Be careful not to use too much, or your color will look like dirty mud or lifeless gray.

A whole book on experiments in dyeing could be written and there have been several excellent leaflets put on the market in the past dozen years. Though written especially for the rug hookers, these are filled with hints which the braider can use to advantage.

Many braiders feel that there is no need to dye. They are the ones who won't even try until they have seen it done with the inevitable result of the better blending of harmonious colors. Only then these doubting Thomases begin to realize that their rugs might have been vastly improved if they were braided of muted or soft gradations of color, instead of the strong, harsh values which they insisted upon putting into their rugs.

Today many of the rug exhibits, which formerly showed hooked rugs only, now feature hooked rugs with braided borders, many all-braided rugs, made with expert dyed harmonies—rugs outstanding as works of real artistic merit which show careful workmanship and original design.

13

WHAT'S IN A NAME?

If you think that it doesn't help a bit to have an individual name for your rug, you're wrong. I have seen more enthusiasm shown when braiders have planned their rugs in advance and have used a little ingenuity and originality with their colors in carrying out the idea of an appropriate name than the ordinary person would dream was possible.

Even the rug which one woman named "RAGS AND TAGS" because she said it was "nothing but leftovers," became a thing of beauty when she began to think of the origin of some of her materials, and that in turn reminded her of the gay and happy times she had when she wore those suits and coats and she began to take more interest in the way she was developing her rug. There were lots of reds and greens, "two colors my husband always liked to see on me."

She made a "HIT-OR-MISS" rug out of her short pieces, and with a little dyeing, had a soft blue-green running in every strand with a beige or gray mixture. In her third strand, she used much red, a little gold and some soft greeny blue. Some of the third strips were made up of many short pieces of various colors and some went the whole round in one color. But as the rug grew, she put in one complete strand of red with her green and her gray mixture and followed this with two greens and a red, then 3 greens followed by another wide section of the "HIT-OR-MISS" type. Two sections were banded this way when I last saw the rug and its maker was ready to enlarge it to another section which would bring the rug to an 8 x 10. When I last saw her, she was buying remnants—those old clothes of hers just didn't stretch far enough. Her friends had contributed so much that she said she felt as if she should change the name to "Friendship." But so much green was needed that she was buying beige in large remnants, and using green to dye it.

Another woman told me she had wanted a new rug for her living room for many years but never could seem to find money enough to buy one. Her husband staked her to $25, "really a birthday and Christmas present too," she confided. She used it to buy materials, attending the rummage sales, begging old clothes from her friends, and purchasing remnants. She made good use of her dye pot which gave her some beautiful shades with very little cost, and finished her 9 x 12 by the goal she had set herself—her 25th wedding anniversary. Do I need to tell you what she called that rug? Yes, it was "SILVER WEDDING." Did it cost more than $25? Yes, even with all her careful planning and buying and her economies in dyeing cloth given to her, the rug cost her $47.50. Had she bought all her materials, that same rug would have cost more than twice that amount. The name she had decided on at the start, had acted as a spur to her endeavors and to her decision to keep down the costs, for her husband had promised a new chair for the living room if she kept the cost under $50. The chair was an anniversary gift, of course.

"FIELDS OF CLOVER" was planned during a trip to a farm. While making this rug, I could just smell the sweetness of that clover with every row I attached. Long after I sold the rug, I had many inquiries for it. "ROSE GARDEN" followed it closely in popularity. "APPLE BLOS- ;OM TIME" is another name which appeals, and the rose and green colors are in all these rugs, a favorite combination.

The autumn colors are now in high favor for floor coverings, to complement the use of the tremendously popular pine, maple and fruitwoods being used in thousands of homes today, especially where there is much casual living.

"OCTOBER SUNSHINE" brings sunny golden days within your home the year 'round. I send countless numbers of the color guides for this rug to the northernmost states, to the farthest south, to the Middle West and the Far West, as well as all over New England, where each fall our hills create this beautiful color array. To a woman in Arkansas who remembered the beautiful autumn colors she saw when she brought her boy to a New England college and who wanted those colors in a rug as a reminder of her wonderful visit, I planned "NEW ENGLAND MEMORIES." For a woman in Pennsylvania who lived a drab existence in a barren home, I planned "SUNSHINE"; to a Maine home where the winters are long and cold, "AUTUMN GLORY" brought warmth and sunshine. To a woman in Florida went "COOL WATERS" in blue greens with only a faint bit of gold to warm it; while "BERKSHIRE HILLS" in its warm golden brown and green tones went to Missouri, and "INDIAN SUMMER" with these same earth tones overshadowed with dusty reds and old golds went to Texas for treasured memories of autumn in New England.

Whether it is the name "COWBOYS AND INDIANS" which attracts, or the fact that it is described as a rug impervious to dirt, many women want guides to that rug for boys' rooms.

"COUNTRY KITCHEN" has been copied more than any rug I have ever made, and I am always hearing of distant places where someone has made it. The fact that the guide lends itself easily to any three contrasting colors makes it an extra popular one to follow.

"SWEET DREAMS" was evolved from soft rose, gray blues, pale green and pale gold and was planned for a girl about to be married. I told her the story behind the colors—the gray blues for an uneventful life before the appearance of Mr. Right, who was represented by the darkest blue. Then the gold was introduced and shortly afterwards, the rose shades. After several rows of these shades depicting the rose-colored glasses with which anyone in love views life, pale green jealousy comes in for a few rows, but soon the "blue" days are over and the rosy days reappear with the deep blue and gold again for an engagement.

Maybe all this planning is foolish to some practical people, but the girl for whom this rug was worked out loved it and tells the story to all her friends. The rug has a double meaning for her. This was the nucleus for several rugs planned for brides to be, and they all wanted a little of these same colors in them. "STARDUST," "BRIDE'S BOUQUET," "SOLDIER'S LEAVE," "CORAL SANDS" and "CONFUSION" were all rugs planned in these same colors for young women about to be married.

"BLUE WILLOW" was patterned after a lovely old tureen of that popular ware and was to be used in a dining room. It was a round rug with much design worked out in various shades of blue with the old blue of the early tureen used constantly. With gray and the dark blue, the many little designs used as in the early oriental rugs gave the rug real distinction.

One woman named her rug "CONFETTI" because she had so many gay colors in it. It was made in a round shape with one strand of black and the two other strands in colors of short pieces. In making a rug of this sort, it is best to braid only a yard or so before lacing it. In this way, you can keep colors adjacent to each other which will blend or complement.

"JOSEPH'S COAT" started out as a quiet rug of only a few colors, but when its maker had a lot of cloth on hand which she couldn't seem to place right, the rug, a square-cornered one, was enlarged and the colors dyed, and a very gay rug resulted and the name, "SOMBER HEELS," was changed to "JOSEPH'S COAT."

"WINTER CARNIVAL" had many green, red and gold designs in arrowheads and diamonds against a background of warm browns.

"EASTER PARADE" was a riot of pastel shades of blue, green, yellow and pink, all tied together with a beige background.

"CHERRY BLOSSOMS" was worked out with cherry red in three values with tweeds dyed in three shades of reseda green and a background of beige and gray tweedy mixture.

"LOVERS' KNOT" was all blues and tans with beige tweed background and gold diamonds worked against the blues and the browns.

"INSPIRATION," "GAY LIFE," "GUESS WORK," "WINTER CHEER," "TOUCH-ME-NOT," "TEMPTATION," "PICKPOCKET," "CHAOS," "AMERICAN LIFE," "DYEING DORA," "FANCY FREE" and such names were all concocted in groups where the whimsy of naming rugs was prevalent and really inspiring, along with the good-natured fun which always is to be found among craftsmen. I am sure that the names were inspirational and expressed many thoughts of the braiders, as well as making the time spent in braiding their rugs pleasant.

14

HINTS FOR TEACHERS
AND COURSE OUTLINE

During a period of several years' teaching and lecturing in New England, New York and New Jersey, I was asked many times to make out a course outline for teachers to follow. In 1954 I gave one at the Fitchburg State Teachers' College in Massachusetts at the Vocational School, and I have given the same course several times to private classes of teachers and would-be teachers. (My pupils have ranged from the tender age of seven to eighty years of age, with the great majority of the women in their middle forties.)

This course outline must necessarily be an elastic one, for while some communities allow 20 lessons of three hours' duration, others permit only 10 three-hour lessons, while some give 20 lessons of but two hours. When the lessons are shorter, allow a little time—not more than 15 minutes—for the laggards to arrive and give your class a talk with board illustrations as soon as you have taken the roll call. If this isn't done at once, you will become involved in individual problems and your evening will be gone before you know it.

With fewer lessons, there must be more class or group and board work and much more homework done by the pupils.

A real craftsman is a potential teacher, for she is always willing and eager to share her knowledge with others. She soon inspires a group of friends, and from this little seed of enthusiasm may come a teacher who in striving to meet the needs of a group, must work out all techniques herself to such a degree that she will be able to solve the problems which so constantly beset the inexperienced braider. As she solves these problems, she grows in stature as a teacher.

A good course in color theory will be of inestimable value to a new teacher. The knowledge of color harmony and balance is necessary in helping beginners plan their rugs. A course in interior decoration will explain how to use colors for rugs against different backgrounds in shape, size and use of rooms, exposure as to light and heat, and of course, the furnishings.

If you feel you would like to teach, start instructing a few friends in your own home, possibly a club or church group. When you feel you are capable of handling a large group, you may want to become a teacher in an Adult Education program. For this, you must prove that you can do good work and are able to find a market for it. You ought to take a course in teacher training which will bring you into contact with other craftsmen like yourself. These lectures, demonstrations and the exchange of ideas do much to give you knowledge, poise and confidence in your ability, as well as in classroom procedure.

With this background and a good course outline of the work you must cover during the sessions of your evening classes, you are ready to face the large groups of braiders and watch them progress from one week to another in the various techniques which you will teach.

Many teachers think of but one thing—a big display at the annual exhibitions. That is a worthy aim, and will probably result in your visitors thinking you are an outstanding teacher. But one who knows all the newer techniques will wonder why so many rugs are just alike—lots of big round ones made no doubt as enlargements of that first chair-seat, and many large continuous oval ones. The techniques for these could surely have been taught in ten lessons and the rugs finished at home.

I believe there should be many "visual" aids which the teacher brings to class which the pupils must study, lesson by lesson, so that with the help of notebooks, they can make a round or an oval or a square-cornered rug when no teacher is at their elbows. These copies should be in every exhibition as part of the pupils' accomplishments even if they don't make quite the impression that the large rugs make.

A chair-seat should be made in three or four lessons—there are always some who will lag behind the others, especially in homework allotted to them. You must have lots of patience in these classes and be prepared for the slow one, the one who is absent and finds it hard to catch up on her work, the one who has already braided and so questions all of your methods as being different from hers, the alert ones who are quiet and go along with you in every step and do all homework without question, and the talkative ones who are so busy whispering to their neighbors that they miss the point of what you are saying and then when they meet that problem, insist that you never told them what to do. There will be left-handed and right-handed women who do things in opposite fashion, clumsy ones who insist they can't braid with folds to the right or the left as you do—have them try both ways and do the one which is easier. There will be those who think dyeing is a waste of time in these days when there is so much material in beautiful colors on the market—they probably will be the very ones who will spend a lot of time after the dyeing lesson in showing off to the class what they have achieved over a week-end by dyeing! Be prepared for variety, not only among your pupils' characters, but in their reaction to instruction and advice and the work they do.

It is really most interesting to watch their progress and their absorption in their work once someone admires it. They need a bit of praise, for new crafts can be difficult and strange and hard on the nerves without someone to project a little humor and encouragement into the serious work.

Train yourself to sketch braids on the blackboard to illustrate certain turns and designs, or have large cardboards with the drawings already made which you can leave on display during the class. Show, with simple blackboard drawings, where increases come on an oval rug, how to space them, where the tapered center ends, where to place butts on ovals or rectangles. These drawings won't tax the sketching ability of anyone and they do make your points clearer.

See that all are provided with either bought or home-made color charts. Don't make them too complicated—the primary and secondary colors are enough, and don't throw words like "analogous" and "juxtaposition" at them. Save those $64 words for later when they understand more about color and the position of one in relation to the other. Teach them color by having them observe. They will soon become extremely conscious of it, for they will be looking at each other's mats and you will be bringing to class various materials, chosen for colors which would blend well in a rug for a certain room.

Various bundles of blending colors with one or two accent colors should be brought in during the first few sessions. More than anything else, the actual materials make your pupils not only color-conscious but alert to the various kinds of cloth which you can use to advantage in a braided rug.

The class given over to dyeing should be an interesting one. In it you can show how to achieve soft greens over gray and white mixtures, or gold over beige and brown mixtures, for these tweedy mixtures are an important part of any large rug.

A word of warning to new teachers: Do not try to teach too much in one night or you will confuse everyone including yourself. One lesson, clearly taught, is far better than several classes of confusion.

If a much larger class appears the first night than you had anticipated, have some strips ready on which they can practice braiding. Never have anyone sitting idle because she has nothing with which to work. Give them cardboard and scissors and have them cut measuring guides or make color guides with crayons which you have provided. Keep them busy and interested until you are ready to call the roll and give your talk. Put yourself heart and soul into that first night. They will respond to your enthusiasm and will not drop out because they think they have wasted their time.

Even if you start with over thirty in your class, you must always take into account the stormy nights, the cold epidemics among the women or members of their families which will result in poor attendance, the few who drop out. But you must keep cheerful while meeting any exigency, be optimistic about the capabilities of all members in your class, make your braiders feel your enthusiasm, and keep a harmonious spirit among them.

Good teachers of rug braiding are in much demand these days and many of the hooking teachers who already know materials, have a good knowledge of dyeing woolens and are dextrous with their hands, are turning to braiding with excellent results.

In the same face-about, rug hooking groups are crowded every year by those who have braided their large rugs and want to use up all their small pieces in making colorful hooked rugs.

Even if your course is not one of the longest, I would still have everyone make a chair-seat for the first project. In a short course, with more group, board and homework, more can be accomplished if all in the class start on the same kind of mat. The technique of turning the center is new and most of the group must be taught how to lace, to increase and to taper off the center. All need instruction in butting. After the chair-seat is made—allow three lessons for this—any project may be started. The chair-seat may easily become a large rug, or the top for a footstool can be made. Or others can be directed in the making of a knitting- or piece-bag for scraps.

By the fourth lesson, you can start them on their samples for the center of an oval rug, with the first bends, the sewing and lacing of the first two braids, and lacing on a straight side. The rectangular rug should be the next project, with each making sharp square ends. Once they have learned these, there is no reason why they can't make any kind of a rug. Mutiple strands are fascinating to most everyone and a little time should be given to showing the simple technique of making these braids. Samples of rugs at every meeting to illustrate the various kinds of rugs are a real drawing-card to a full attendance.

A large canvas duffle bag, such as those golfers and sailors use, holds many of the numerous things a teacher must always carry along with her if she is to maintain a sustained interest in her classes. She should always have with her such essentials as threads of various colors and extra needles, T pins and safety pins, clothespins, extra braid holders, swatches of cloth, her color guide, extra note paper and pencils, colored crayons, scissors, pliers. Someone is always forgetting something and your prepared box should be an open sesame of good will. Don't let the privilege be abused. But the happier you can keep these women and the busier and the more effort *you* put into your work, the better will be the response.

course outline

This course outline is primarily for teachers in adult education where the groups are large and the numbers of teaching hours are set for you. It can be shortened by omitting much of the individual instruction, the unusual rugs, by having the chair-seat made as a sample of a round rug, a stair-tread as a sample of an oval, and a rectangular top for a footstool made to show the square-cornered techniques. With more homework, you can still have a fine exhibition at the close of the session in which to show a variety of work accomplished.

Classes held privately are usually small and can be much more informal. They may last three hours, or there may be an all day session with a half-hour break for lunch. Each member brings a sandwich and each takes her turn in providing a simple dessert such as cake or cookies. The hostess furnishes tea or coffee.

In these groups, although there can be far more individual work, nevertheless a routine should be followed, with talks, demonstrations and visual aids made by everyone, to show certain techniques.

Lesson 1: Teacher should arrive early every night and have her samples of little rugs in different shapes spread out on desk or table. Some will arrive with empty hands that first night, and you must keep these busy if you are to retain their interest. See that your rugs show various color harmonies or distinctive designs.

The first night the teacher will be laden with the rug samples plus all the samples of equipment, such as thread, braid holders, safety pins, braid-aids, bundles of materials of many colors, textures and weights, some—ready to use—in strips showing the proper width for the weight. And if possible, have one or two bundles of cloth of harmonious shades which you can hold up over your arm to show colors which may be used together in a rug. With the present-day popularity of maple furniture, a bundle which will appeal to many will be made up of beige, tans, golden and spice browns, rusts and gold. You can add blue for accent or, taking that out, put in some bronze or olive green. When you see the nods of approval as you hold this up, you realize it was well worth the effort of accumulating the materials just for show reasons, even though you had to dye several pieces to make the color harmony.

As the class assembles, they can be looking at these bundles and at the rugs which you have on display. When all are there, and you have had them remove their wraps, let them stand in a semicircle if possible and as you call the roll, have each one tell where she lives. They will be interested in seeing their fellow workers and learning if any live near enough to form "pools" to drive back and forth to class. Neighbors who never have before seen each other have come to be close friends because of these classes.

If you have already been given the list of those who are expected, you have their telephone numbers as well as addresses and at a later class, before the bad weather sets in, you may want to form a sort of round robin telephone system for letting everyone know if, for any reason, a class is to be omitted.

While they are still in a semicircle, hold up the rugs, one at a time, so that all may see them. Chair-seats and footstool covers and stair-treads may be passed around. This is the time to tell them the rules of the school and those governing their attendance at class.

Do not keep them standing too long. They want to accomplish something definite that first night. You explain the equipment and where they can find it and then set everyone to making measuring guides from the cardboards you have brought with you. Shirtboards are a good weight for this. Rulers, scissors, pencils are passed around quickly as you move about the group to look at the equipment which some of them have brought and to pass on their materials. Be prepared to see good, bad, soiled, moth-eaten, thin, thick, fine, coarse cloth of all sorts.

Explain that for the first project, each one must make a chair-seat, and give the reasons for this mat. Explain that while they are making it, they will be accumulating their woolens for their large rug and that they are to keep their eyes open to the color all around them. Explain that all errors can be made on a chair-seat but that when they are making their large rugs, they will not want to ruin expensive materials by practicing on them. Being adult, they will readily understand why.

Housekeepers (usually two) are appointed at each lesson to see that the room is left in good condition when the class is over. Each person must pick up any scraps of cloth around her place but the housekeepers will check at the last moment.

At the halfway mark of the lesson, allow a five-minute break. If the teacher wears sensible clothes and comfortable shoes, the pupils will follow suit. Lint gathers quickly, so a smock is always in good taste when attending a class.

After your five-minute recess, all will have their measuring guides ready, and some will have their strips torn for the first braid. This should be a straight practice braid and should be checked on by the teacher when it is not more than 6-8 inches long. Start all with finger-and-thumb method, unless they have the braid-aids with them and want to use them. If they are not too adept with their fingers, let them try a set of the braid-aids which you should have in your box of supplies. In about fifteen minutes, you will have checked the entire class with the braid. Do not try to enclose ends or make the "sore thumb" start until you check on everyone's braid. Now take out any unsatisfactory beginnings and help do the braid until it is a small, neat, uniform one. Put that aside and start with a fresh piece if you have the cloth; otherwise, unbraid, and use the same strips.

Show by drawing on the board, how to do the "sore thumb" start and have all do it for the beginning of the chair-seat. Now show the modified square corner for the center. Some will finish the little center that evening, so you can have a sample of a tapered end to pass around, explaining the ending of the center.

It is best to ask everyone to start a braid with the strand at the right of a safety pin and keep the open folds also on the right. This will make it easier for you when you are teaching how to butt. However, you will have some in the class who will do this from the left, and you must work this out yourself so as to be able to give correct directions.

Give out the homework before the end of the class—all centers to be completed and the braid for the next two rows made with enclosed ends. This method is easy to show and may be used right at the beginning instead of the "sore thumb" enclosure.

Announce that the second lesson will be on lacing and tapering.

Lesson 2: Check on all centers and homework. Teach sewing the center by use of the blunted darning needle which can act as a lacer. Teach lacing with increases to keep the mat symmetrical. Teach a square knot.

Some will have more than two braids made to go around the mat, but most of them will sew and lace their centers and taper off during the evening.

Homework—have them make enough straight braids (six or seven) to finish the mat. There will be a few slow ones who will not finish the tapering.

Lesson 3: Review braiding a straight braid, tapering and lacing. Majority will be ready to lace on the loose straight braids. Teach butting. Some will do two braids, others only one. Board drawings will help.

Homework—let them lace on the other braids, butting each row.

Lesson 4: Some of the mats will appear all finished with six or seven butted rows. All mats should be finished in this class. Talk on color harmony, showing a color chart, and let those who have finished their mats, make charts. Use simple terms in speaking of shades of the same color ranging from light to dark—light, medium and dark—so they will understand your terminology. Speak of "neighboring" colors and opposites. Pass around the dye chart put out by Cushing Perfection Dyes and point out related shades. They can understand a color guide like this and when you announce that the next lesson will be on dyeing, their interest will be aroused.

Homework—all finished mats to be ready for display at next meeting. Materials to be gathered for a large rug.

Lesson 5: This one is on dyeing and should be an actual demonstration. If you cannot have the use of a kitchen, perhaps a laboratory may be available. Even if you carry along a two-burner plate and a couple of basins, it is far more effective to let your pupils see the actual steps involved in the process. While the dyes are cooking you can explain the ease and the beauty of the finished products. Show the difference in the absorption of dye by tweeds and by materials like suedes. Explain how tweedy mixtures can be thickened up and become vastly more interesting with a weak dye. Keep note of how much dye is used in the batch you have simmering on the stove, and show how to keep results in your notebook so you can match it if needed. Explain the use of salt or vinegar to set dyes, the need of constant stirring for even dyeing, and the effect of too much crowding in the dye pot.

Half of your lesson will be devoted to the work and talk on dyeing. You can use the second half in teaching how to plan enough materials for the large rug you want to make, the length of the center braid and so on.

All new rugs should be started at this class, with a straight braid and the enclosed beginning. Review the modified bend for those making an oval and teach the sharp square corner for those starting a rectangle or square rug.

Teach putting the first two braids together and how to go around the safety pin to where you lace straight without any skips. For those who will work at home, show by board work where the increases will come, on the curves in threes, on the ovals, and by merely skipping the one in corners on rectangles. Now you can say, "Work for yourself now, going as fast as you wish."

Lesson 6: A general review of techniques learned in Lesson 5 must be conducted. Check for straight centers, straight sides, particularly square-cornered rugs. Check for three safety pins along the center line of each of these rugs to help keep the sides straight and the corners right-angled.

Review by board work, the increases on ends of ovals and on individual rugs by putting ends to ends to watch for even and symmetrical curves.

Homework—complete centers for rugs.

Lesson 7: Explain how to add new color in a continuous braid. Repeat instructions on increases. Have each pupil start her own color guide.

Homework—bring in a possible color guide for whole rug.

Lesson 8: Patterns or designs in rugs. Have rugs to show the various little patterns, and show by board work just how they are worked out. Check on color guides. Homework will now go as fast as the pupil's enthusiasm will allow her to work.

Lesson 9: Devote half the lesson to making samples of the various techniques which you have taught, the rest of the time to checking progress on large projects.

Homework—bring to next class all finished visual aids and all finished mats for "Open House."

Lesson 10: Open House. If there are to be ten more lessons, this exhibition may be postponed. Some may be enlarging their chair-seats into rugs and those who have not finished their visual aids will be working on them.

Lesson 11: Do not expect any work done on rugs during the holidays. All appear at this lesson with somewhat blank memories, and you must be understanding and review much of what was taught during the first ten lessons.

Lesson 12: These winter months will find many absent and you can give more individual work, with help on increases and butting and color harmony taking up much of the teaching period. The large rugs will continue to grow, and some will want to copy the two or three circle rugs which were begun with a chair-seat. All seem to want to make the footstool covers and are anxious to have several projects under way.

Unusual rugs: show different type rugs. Some always want to start a stair carpet or a rug with points. Be sure they are equal to the demands of good workmanship in these rugs before you allow them to start. By this time, women making large rugs should have their color guides made up, so that they can leave their big rugs at home if they are butted. If a rug has been continuous up to this time, the braider can taper off and butt for the rest of the rows.

Lesson 13: I like to tell something about the old rugs of early days, and so about this time comes a lesson when you can give a short talk on the history of the braided rug in its various forms. I have been surprised more than once to have an absentee who has heard about the talk ask if I could possibly give it again so that all might hear it. After the talk, I have had many very old rugs appear and the whole class has been interested in examining them. The talk takes only about 15 minutes but it does offer interesting knowledge to a rug braider.

Lesson 14: Many who have made large scatter oval or round rugs are now starting a rectangle, and often it is a "Hit-or-Miss" rug which may be under way as a means for using up the scraps left after the large rug was completed. Instruction on color harmonies continues and colored pictures are often brought to class to illustrate the talks.

Lesson 15: By this time, everyone should have completed her mat and a scatter rug. Materials may be hard to find and you should give your class a list of various mills which have remnant rooms, mill-end stores, and remnant shops where they may find suitable woolens. If there is a class in rug hooking in progress in the same school, try to arrange with the instructor for a short visit from your class. There they see what they can do with their left-over pieces and the effect of the dyes. This latter will give a decided impetus to their dyeing in case they have been lagging along with this technique.

Lesson 16: This is the time to recheck each pupil to see that she is really getting the most out of your instruction. Note how many rows are added each week. Some always appear with excuses, but there are others too reticent about their inability to understand all the new terms and too timid to ask you to repeat. You must follow up these slower braiders or they will become discouraged and drop out. In the second session of your course, they are the ones who will take up your time. You teach all the essential techniques in the first ten lessons. In the second ten, you review and teach again for the ones who are slower at grasping this new craft.

Lesson 17: What do you expect by this time in your class? Can you as a teacher really take a breathing spell? No, for now when they are making their color guides, you will find that many braiders will not dye a piece of cloth or add a new color unless you advise it. These workers need more lessons on color and this you give. Now you can talk about your analogous colors, your complementaries and split complementaries and use the terms "chroma" and "value" and so on. With the frequent use of these words throughout the course, the workers begin to have a much better understanding of the relationship of colors. They will better understand the effect of bright red in a rug instead of cool greens. They will notice by looking at the other rugs being made around them how designed rugs with soft harmony can be achieved with few colors but many dyed shades. This lesson can be given from the eleventh lesson on, for no lesson is complete without a little instruction in the use of color in the home as a background for an individual personality.

Lesson 18: If a pupil has not made progress by now, she won't make much of a rug. In addition to that chair-seat, she should have a large rug nearing completion or two scatter rugs nearly finished. If each row has been butted, we do not expect the rug to be as large as that of a continuous braid.

In 20 lessons a class of energetic rug makers can have finished several 9 ft. rounds from chair-seats, 6 x 9 three-circle rugs, 8 x 10 butted ovals, 9 x 12 rugs completed with continuous braids and the last one or two butted, a 6 x 13 square-cornered rug, a 3 x 5 butted one, a 3 x 5 ft. butted oval and a 3 x 5 butted rectangle.

In these last lessons, be sure that everyone has the visual aids as samples to which they can refer after the classes are over, when the urge to braid a different kind of rug than the ones made in class overtakes them.

Lesson 19: This is given over to last minute color guides which are not complete for large rugs. If these color guides are made out for the room-sized rugs under way, your pupils will feel more confident about being able to finish them alone. If some of the material was dyed, check their notebooks to see if they have the "recipe" for dyeing another batch. Check all curves of the ovals, see that the last butted rows are put on as a good finish. Send everyone away with the happy knowledge that they can bring good-looking rugs to the final exhibition the next week.

Lesson 20: Though this lesson takes the form of an exhibition for the public, you may work extra hours in helping to set it up and to be on hand when last minute rugs appear. You may be staying long after the exhibit has closed to give extra help to someone deciding after she has seen all the other rugs, that she will start another one immediately. Give her the help she needs, because a few extra minutes of your time now may mean hours of pleasure to her later on. A teacher is happy when she gives. Much of what she has given may come back to her through the years. Remember you may be an inspiration to a future teacher who will carry on your work!

15

THE GRACIOUS YEARS—
THERAPEUTIC VALUE OF CRAFTS

Our hairs may turn gray and our chins may grow double,
But we'll braid our own rugs so we'll keep out of trouble,
Our colors are gay and so are our hearts
We'll braid and we'll lace 'til we finish our charts.

One very stormy winter's night, when out of a class of twenty only eight women had appeared, I gave much of my time to each individual in helping her make out a color chart for her particular rug. The group was made up almost entirely of the older members of the class, but they seemed to feel well repaid for venturing out into the storm. (My groups, by the way, have always ranged in age from around twenty to seventy years of age.) Most of these women had families grown up enough to be left alone, so that the husbands could drive the women to class and call for them later—as simple as that. The men-folk were very proud of the rugs they were making, to say nothing of the money they were saving by not buying new rugs to replace the worn-out ones in their homes.

They were a gay crowd that night without the young group to overshadow them, and line by line and with a lot of good-natured banter, they improvised the above rhyme. I wrote it down and have thought so many times of the chatter which revealed the stories behind their rugs. One of the oldest women had had a siege of arthritis, but she loved the braiding because there were so many different things to be done that no one set of muscles was ever exhausted. (She never missed one of the lessons.) Then there was the usually tight-lipped woman whose husband seemed to spend most of his time playing cards. This was her one "night out" and her braiding was filling a tremendous gap in her life. There were two women who had just happened to sit side by side the first night and so discovered they were near neighbors—they always came together now and seemed to be close friends. Then there was the little grandmother who was making two bedside rugs for her grandchildren out west. She was very lonesome now that her only daughter had moved so many miles away, and making the rugs was filling a big void in her life. There was a younger woman whose husband had recently accepted a teaching position with a western college in the Middle West. She planned to have braided rugs all over her home, no matter where she might be living. Maybe she is teaching some of her Mid-Western neighbors some of the techniques she learned back in New England.

There are many people all over this land of ours who feel lost and forlorn as the years speed along. This is especially true after the children have left the family nest and the cares of the home lessen. Too many women feel out of things, neglected, or not needed, and in the winter months especially, time hangs heavily on their hands. All these electrical and mechanical devices are wonderful time-savers for the housewife but what to do with all the extra time they give us? Early retirement from work is another factor which must be considered.

Craft centers, adult education classes, home bureaus, state extension services, Y.W.C.A.s, church and private classes in handicrafts are solving innumerable cases of boredom, loneliness and idle hours, as well as for those who suffer from tensions, grief, sadness at the loss of a loved one, separation from dear friends or relatives, loss of lower limbs, or failing eyesight. All these contribute to the ever-increasing numbers of mature men and women who join groups for instruction in rug braiding. And in addition to the above, one explanation most encountered among people of all ages is that they are looking for an escape from the ordinary routine of everyday life into a creative world where something beautiful and practical may be made, mutual interests may be shared, and a prized possession may be created for the admiration of husband, friends and relatives. These rugs are our own individual expression of art and the glow of accomplishment lingers for years. Braided rugs grow fast, do not require too much skill to produce, and the work is very easy on the eyes.

For those who suffer from arthritis in wrists and arms, I always give a bit of warning: Don't let your enthusiasm run away with you. Do a little braiding at a time. Don't try to keep up with that young bundle of energy and good health sitting beside you. Unused muscles need a limbering-up. Gradually you'll have more strength and less pain. Many different steps are required to make a braided rug, and it is not necessary to stay in one position for any length of time.

If we use old clothing, it must be torn up, washed, perhaps dyed, stripped by hand or machine, with the strips sewn together. As we braid, we stop to lace and constantly adjust our braids. These may all sound like trivial things, but they do need motions with different sets of muscles, and you can do these various operations sitting at a table, standing up, walking around as you braid, or you can use a standing braid holder and lean back in your comfortable armchair and braid as you watch your favorite television program. All sorts of gadgets and good lacing thread make the accomplishment of a hand-braided rug a far quicker and easier operation than those made by an earlier generation.

I know one woman and her daughter who divide the work. The daughter buys the new material or haunts the rummage sales, prepares it, does the stripping and dyeing, and plans the colors. From that point, the mother takes over for the braiding and lacing.

Many a man does all the lacing for his wife, and one woman I knew was always in a rush to keep her braids ahead of her husband's desire to do more and more lacing. Hers was a room-sized rug and she was butting each row. She was hard put to it to keep ahead of him until I suggested that she keep four braids going at once. Since each is butted on a different curve—and if she started each one for him—he could lace until it was time for her to do the joining, and as she did that, he could be lacing on another round. I often keep four braids going at once. It is a tremendous saving of pulling the rug around if the space on which you work is cramped.

One man had flatly refused to become interested in helping his wife with either the braiding or the lacing. One night when she had been out to a party, she came home to a real surprise. Cosily ensconced in his favorite chair was the man of the house, surrounded by yards of braid. From that time on, he and his wife made all their rugs together.

Many men are loath to take lessons with a group of women, but several have come to me for private instruction while others have sent their wives for the information which was then passed on to them in the privacy of their homes.

A man telephoned me one day to ask if I would take his wife into one of my classes. They had lived in the town for over a year, but she was an unusually timid little woman and had made no friends and her husband was afraid of a nervous breakdown. Of course I took her. People with common interest in handicrafts are no snobs. They are friendly, neighborly and talkative. At the opening session of all my classes, I always quote from James Russell Lowell's "Vision of Sir Launfal":

It's not what we give, but what we share,
For the gift without the giver is bare;
Who gives himself with his alms feeds three,
Himself, his hungry neighbor and Me.

That particular woman found two neighbors at the first meeting on whom she had never laid eyes. She soon became a member of their "Neighbors' Coffee Club," and today she is a far different woman from the shrinking violet who sat in the very last seat of my class that first night. She braided several rugs, then at my suggestion took up hooking since she had enough pretty woolens for several hooked mats left over from the braiding. She had learned enough about colors and dyeing to take to the hooking with ease, and now she is an ardent hooker.

After only a few lessons, I am generally informed on all sides that my pupils have become instructors for their aunts, grandmothers, sisters and neighbors. This goes on every year like the ever-widening ripples which appear when you throw a pebble into a pool of water. I must be one of the country's greatest grandmothers in terms of braiding instructions, for my pupils' pupil's pupils are now teaching in various parts of New England, as far out as the West Coast and down into the Deep South.

When I lecture before clubs, craft groups, church organizations or various gatherings of handicrafters, I find my listeners most eager for the actual demonstrations of the new techniques. Most women will read over directions for any kind of needlecraft without at first grasping the full meaning of the terms. But let them see the process actually done by someone, and lo! It is like a jigsaw puzzle—one or two pieces in place, and you can understand the over-all picture in no time at all and find the proper pieces without any difficulty.

Bringing these groups of ruggers together makes for a satisfying gathering. In no time, everyone is talking to someone she never saw before, discussing the best places to buy woolens, the width and thickness and firmness of braids, colors which are so hard to find and how to obtain them through dyeing, oval rugs versus rectangular ones, stair-treads versus stair carpets, odd-shaped rugs, and all the varied topics which are to be heard wherever there are groups of rug braiders. Through this mutual hobby, they plan to visit exhibitions together, and all the while a general feeling of friendship prevails.

The annual Hooking and Braiding Bee at Storrowton is a good example of this kind of gathering. Until 1954, it was strictly only a Hooking Bee, with hundreds of hookers from many states coming to the Village Green of this old re-created New England village, with the original old buildings transplanted from various old Colonial settlements. The buildings are within the grounds of the New England Exposition which covers many acres at West Springfield, Massachusetts. The Bee takes place on the last Thursday of July and is open free of charge to anyone interested in these crafts. It lasts all day and women who come bring their choice rugs for others to see. Those chosen as outstanding in their class are exhibited at the Eastern States Exposition in September.

When I was asked in 1954 to show my unusual rugs, especially those with hooked centers, and to tell what I was doing to raise standards of braided rugs, I showed examples of the old primitive rugs with lots of bright colors and plenty of black, blended traditional rugs, contemporary rugs with few colors subtly harmonizing, and strictly modern rugs with outstanding patterns.

The rug hookers showed so much enthusiasm over all the rugs that countless new friendships were made on the spot. Many of the women told me they were yearning to make room-sized braided rugs. "Hooked rugs are beautiful but do take so long to make and are hard on the eyes," was their constant cry. Would I help them? I would and have, and many of them are now excellent braiding teachers as well as hooking instructors.

I admitted that I had stolen one of their ideas. I named my rugs. It came about this way. During one winter several years ago, I had been knitting argyle socks steadily, besides plaiting a 9 x 11 rug with ½ inch-wide flat braids, all of which were sewn together with Aunt Lydia's linen thread without a stitch showing. Anyone who has done this knows what a wreck it makes of your fingers. The needle and thread cut through the flesh, callouses are formed. You put on heavy kid gloves or even fingers cut from them, and then you keep taking them off because your hands become too warm. This went on until late spring and then I was really very foolish and overworked my hands and arms by removing the paper from four bedrooms so that they might be re-papered while we were away in Maine for the summer.

I really brought on bursitis and arthritis through my own energy and overexertion and so decided I would turn to the round braids at once. They required far less effort and could be laced instead of sewn. I made the braids a bit wider and found that it was considerably easier work in this fashion and the braids went much faster. Because it was the rug made while I still had arthritis, I called it "OLD ARTHRITIS." Many a pupil suffering from this handicap takes great comfort in looking at this rug and seeing the possibilities which lie within herself for accomplishment. Did I have the arthritis and bursitis very long? About six months, but I always used the arm a little bit every day.

The well-laced rug today, with its sturdy interlocked loops and its blended harmony of color and small designs to lend interest, is a far cry from the crudely made rugs of the early 19th century, yet the charm and glow of richly subdued colors, and the warmth and cheer which one always feels with a good woolen braided rug underfoot, continue to fascinate and draw more and more craftsmen into the ranks of ruggers. A little wool, good use of spare time, the desire to create an individual floor covering—and before you realize it, your little mat has become a beautiful, eye-catching, room-sized rug.

Your real or imaginary troubles have vanished into the past, you welcome a few hours to work by yourself, and you are so engrossed that you wish you had more time to work on your rug. Tensions lessen and boredom is forgotten. A simple creative craft has made a different woman out of you.

16
CARE AND CLEANING
OF BRAIDED RUGS

If you have made your rug with care, you should treat it as you would any fine wool floor covering, so that it will give you comfort and joy for years.

If your materials are firm and strong and the braids are closely interlocked, you can use a sweeper on it every day or your vacuum cleaner once or twice a week, just as you do on any other rug in your home. It needs no special attention.

We no longer pick up our mats and take them out-of-doors and shake or beat them. They are firmly interlocked and have a smooth enough surface which is cleaned thoroughly with the suction of the vacuum cleaner. You may pick up small rugs and take them out doors and sweep them with a corn broom if you wish. This will get down into any dirt pockets you may have. Do them on the grass if possible, first on one side, then on the other.

Shaking and beating rugs hanging on a line will very likely put too much of a strain on the lacing thread, and if your mats were not closely interlocked, they may stretch out of shape and the thread may break. Broken threads can be mended with a fresh piece, by tieing at both ends with a square knot, but let's avoid the necessity for this mending if possible.

Rugs which I sewed twenty-five years ago have never had a stitch replaced, even though they have been used constantly during the years. Rugs with the over-and-over stitches which show on the wrong side—I made the variety which went through the cloth and were entirely invisible—do wear out and give out sooner.

If you find a worn spot in your rug, remove the strands and replace them. If you have learned to butt, it will not be any chore for you. A woman who dropped a lighted cigarette on her rug, failed to notice it until the rug was burned badly. Before she came to class the following week, she had removed the burned section, and replaced the two damaged braids with two pieces butted so carefully that her story was somewhat doubted until she proudly pointed out the new pieces. She was fortunate indeed to have had materials on hand which matched the old ones perfectly.

A rug which had been used for almost five years was finally enlarged to a 9 x 12 for use in a larger room. It had never been used on the right side, waiting for the time when it might be enlarged. A thick lather of Lux Flakes dissolved in a basin of warm water with a little ammonia added to it, was used to scrub the surface of the rug, the suds wiped off with a clean wet towel and the rug looked as fresh as ever.

When you clean a large rug this way, do it in sections, a few square feet at a time, so that the suds do not stay on the rug for a long time. A tablespoon of borax or ammonia will help to restore colors. Have a second basin of warm water with a turkish towel to wipe off the suds. If the rug is too large to take out of doors, choose a warm, sunny, windy day and keep your windows open so that the rug will dry in as short a time as possible.

If there are spots or stains on the rug, I use Barcolene which is a dry cleaning agent I use on my oriental rugs and on my upholstery as well. Work fast and out on the porch or on the grass.

When your rug becomes too soiled for home cleaning, send it to a good dry-cleaning establishment. After a year of college life with one of my boys, I did not recognize the rug which he brought back with him as one I had made. A trip to the dry-cleaner and I knew it was the one I had made.

A woman who lives in the Naugatuck River Valley in Connecticut had the lower floor of her home covered with silt and water to a depth of three feet during the August 1955 floods. She told me that when the waters had receded and she saw the sodden mass of what had been her lovely 9 x 12 ft. living room braided rug, she thought it was a complete loss. However, she sent it to a cleaner and was agreeably surprised to have the rug returned to her looking brighter and more beautiful than it did before the flood.

Not so fortunate was a woman in Massachusetts whose summer home was filled with exceptionally well-made rugs. They just disappeared, house and all the furnishings, in a tidal wave!

Do keep your rugs clean and free from dirt and grime. It is the dirt which falls on the surface and which is allowed to stay there that eventually sifts through the cloth and cuts the fibers.

If there is a place in your home which has a lot of traffic, keep the rug turned as to corners and to the wrong and the right sides so that the wear will be equalized. Small rugs should be turned over often. After all we make our rugs reversible so that they can have added wear. We want them to be long-lived after all the work we have put into them. So take care of them and make them work for you too.

If the weather is bad, turn them over to the wrong side so muddy boots or shoes won't track them up with dirt. Keep rubber carpeting under them to avoid accidents, especially if there are children who do so much running around. This rubber carpeting will save wear on the rug too, for it is softer than wood.

Woolen braids as they are walked upon, flatten out and if you are careless and make large braids, remember you'll have even larger ones as the rug is used. Start with smaller braids. Even though it may take you a little longer to complete your rug, you will always be happy with it. It is the rugs made with the tiny braids which have survived the years. You want your rugs to be prized heirlooms some day, so make them well and care for them diligently.

17

FORGET ME NOTS—
IMPORTANT REMINDERS

1   Open your eyes to color and plan a rug before you start it.
2   Your rug will be as good as the materials and workmanship you put into it and the way you arrange your colors.
3   Think of these three words as you work: observe—remember—compare.
4   Save your little triangles to make your color guide.
5   Make small braids which will be admired as heirlooms.
6   Enclose the raw edges before you begin to braid.
7   Keep a medium-sized safety pin at the start of your braid, turn it over to the wrong side when you lace, and keep it there until the rug is finished.
8   Learn to braid and lace with an even tension.
9   Braid on the right side; lace on the wrong side. This will save time and motion. Keep the body of the rug away from you as you lace.
10   Treat the curves of an oval rug like the two halves of a circle.
11   Space your increases at different places each row and mark with T pins.
12   Make three increases on each shoulder of a curved end.
13   Three increases bring back the little patterns with which you make designs.
14   Never skip a loop on the straight sides of oval or rectangular rugs.
15   Interlock your loops, one between the other, to give the new woven look to your rugs.
16   Make the first two bends in an oval rug with the modified square corners.
17   Make the center of a round rug with a succession of modified square corners.

18 A sharp square corner requires three turns over from the left before the strand from the right is pulled over the middle.

19 If possible, learn to pull over the strand at your right first when you start a braid. This will help you later when you butt the row.

20 Keep the open folds on your right if possible, especially if you use braid-aids.

21 In working with multiple strands, to keep the design correct when making straight braids, start to braid from the left. For each successive braid to match, the strand at the farthest right moves to the farthest left for each new row.

22 Safety pin points to the shoulder of the curve where colors change in a spiral rug, or taper off for the center of a butted rug; where a spiral rug is ended and to the first corner of a squared rug.

23 Attach new colors so that they appear on the outside edge of the right side of the braid.

24 Use three to five dyed shades of one color for harmoniously blended rugs.

25 Use plenty of tweeds, especially in continuous braids.

26 Patterns are formed by using contrasting colors against each other in regular formation.

27 Put in patterns for accents and for distincti   rugs.

28 For the love of your rug, dye and dye often. Stir often to obtain clear colors.

29 Brilliant colors are good only for accent, but not in quantity except in "hit-or-miss" rugs.

30 Save your recipes for dyeing; you may need them later.

31 "Hit-or-miss" rugs are more distinctive with one strand of color, one strand of black, and one strand of gray or beige mixture.

32 Concentric circles of a solid dark color tend to make your rug look smaller.

33 Square-cornered rugs are very satisfactory made with a continuous braid; the only loops skipped are the ones on each corner which you pull tight from the right.

34 Do not braid beyond a corner until you lace, to make sure of the spot where you will square it.

35 Pressing on the wrong side with a wet cloth and a hot iron will

take out minor troubles, but if this doesn't make your rug lie flat, unbraid and do it over.

36 Ripples on a straight side may be caused by a larger braid being attached to a small one. Don't be in such a hurry. Take it out and make a braid as uniformly wide as the ones you have been making.

37 Keep the rug flat on a table as you work and on the floor when you are not working on it.

38 Make turns for square corners in your fingers; it is the only way you can pull Strand 3 tight enough.

39 Don't try to cut all your material at once. You may decide you need it narrower or wider after you have braided a while.

40 Keep a scrap book with all your dyeing experiments noted and pictures of all the pretty braided rugs you see in magazines.

41 Attend exhibitions of both hooked and braided rugs. You are bound to find inspiration from the rugs.

18
A LIST OF RUGS

APPLE BLOSSOM TIME

Rectangle, butted, 31 x 49 rug, modified square corners, squared in the braid. 18 in. center. Center simulates trunk of an apple tree, then come rows of all green "leaves," separating "apple blossom" rows, with shades of pink and rose used for the flowers as two strands, while the third strand of bronze green (dyed over beige with speck of bright green added) becomes the center for each flower, in rows 8-9, 11-12, 14-15, and 17-18.

The greens in the last three rows, if field or khaki green is used, can be overdyed with scarlet or turkey red in a weak solution to give a gray or reddish brown. Greens separating the flower rows are better if beige tweeds are overdyed with bronze and bright greens to give the effect of different shades of greens in the leaves.

This rug was copied by a woman in Wisconsin who said the original made her think of her apple orchard in the spring.

ROWS 1-4 — 1 field green (khaki), 1 greenish brown, 1 tan

ROW 5 — 1 field green, 1 light brown, 1 reseda or gray green

ROWS 6-7 — 1 light green, 1 gray green, 1 light brown

ROWS 8-9 — 2 medium rose, 1 light green, keep greens against each other when lacing

ROW 10 — 3 shades of green

ROWS 11-12 — 1 light rose, 1 dark rose, 1 green

ROW 13 — 3 shades of green

ROWS 14-15 — 1 light rose, 1 dark rose, 1 green

ROW 16 — 3 shades of green

ROWS 17-18 — 2 medium rose, 1 green

ROW 19 — 3 shades of green

ROW 20 — 2 greens, 1 light brown

ROWS 21-22 — 1 field green, 1 brown, 1 greenish brown

ROW 23 — 1 field green, 1 grayish brown, 1 reddish brown

ROW 24 — 1 field green, 1 grayish brown, 1 lt. brown

AUTUMN GLORY

Oval rug, 7 x 8, continuous to 5 x 6; all other rows butted. Rug made by Dorothy Putnam of Worcester, teacher outstanding in that area. It is in the home of Mrs. Putnam's daughter, Mrs. Henry Boynton of Hartford, Conn. It is a fine blended rug in excellent taste with the old pine and maple furniture with which it is used.

Beige, brown, and mixtures of these same colors are used as background for this rug. Mrs. Putnam used as dyes, 3 parts old gold and 1 part mummy brown over yellow, which gave her the lovely gold shades in five gradations; for her rusts, she has five shades obtained by using rust dye over light pink. Three shades of yellow greens were dyed, using 3 parts bronze green and one part bright green over beige.

Center: 1-foot-long rows 1-5 — 1 taupe, 2 beige and brown mixture. Keep same colors against each other when lacing, for diagonals, arrowheads and ric-rac.

ROW 6 — 2 taupe, 1 beige and brown mix.
ROW 7 — 2 taupe, 1 light green
ROW 8 — 1 taupe, 1 light green, 1 darker green
ROW 9 — 1 taupe, 2 darker green
ROW 10 — 1 brown, 2 darker green
ROW 11 — 2 brown, 1 darker green
ROW 12 — 2 brown, 1 mixture (same colors against each other when lacing)
ROW 13 — 1 brown, 2 mixture
ROW 14 — 1 brown, 1 mixture, 1 beige
ROW 15 — 1 brown, 2 beige
ROW 16 — 2 brown, 1 beige (lacing to form ric-rac)
ROW 17 — 1 brown, 2 beige
ROW 18 — 2 beige, 1 gold No. 1 (lightest shade)
ROW 19 — 1 beige, 1 gold No. 1, 1 gold No. 2
ROW 20 — 1 beige, 2 gold No. 2
ROW 21 — 1 beige, 1 gold No. 2, 1 gold No. 3
ROW 22 — 1 brown, 1 gold No. 2, 1 gold No. 3
ROW 23 — 1 brown, 1 gold No. 3, 1 gold No. 4
ROW 24 — 1 brown, 1 gold No. 4, 1 gold No. 5
ROW 25 — 2 brown, 1 shade gold No. 5
ROW 26 — 2 brown, 1 beige
ROW 27 — 1 brown, 2 beige (same colors against each other for ric-rac)
ROW 28 —2 brown, 1 beige
ROW 29 — 1 brown, 1 beige, 1 rust No. 1
ROW 30 — 1 beige, 1 rust No. 1, 1 rust No. 2
ROW 31 — 2 rust No. 1, 1 rust No. 2
ROW 32 — 1 rust No. 1, 2 rust No. 2
ROW 33 — 2 rust No. 2, 1 rust No. 3
ROW 34 — 1 rust No. 2, 1 rust No. 3, 1 rust No. 4
ROW 35 — 2 rust No. 3, 1 rust No. 4
ROW 36 — 1 rust No. 3, 2 rust No. 4
ROW 37 — 2 rust No. 4, 1 rust No. 5

ROW 38 — 2 rust No. 5, 1 brown and beige mix., making double ric-
rac

ROW 39 — 1 rust No. 5, 2 brown and beige mix.

ROW 40 — 2 rust No. 5, 1 brown and beige mix.

ROW 41 — 1 rust No. 5, 2 brown and beige mix.

ROW 42 — 1 brown, 1 beige mix.

ROWS 43-44 — 1 brown, 1 mix — Rat-tail first of these rows

ROWS 44-45 — 2 brown, 1 beige

ROW 46 — 1 brown, 2 beige

ROW 47 — 1 brown, 1 beige, 1 gold No. 1

ROW 48 — 1 brown, 1 gold No. 1, 1 gold No. 2

ROW 49 — 1 brown, 2 gold No. 2

ROW 50 — 1 brown, 1 gold No. 2, 1 gold No. 3

ROW 51 — 1 brown, 2 gold No. 3

ROW 52 — 1 brown, 1 gold No. 3, 1 gold No. 4

ROW 53 — 1 brown, 2 gold No. 4

ROW 54 — 1 brown, 1 gold No. 4, 1 gold No. 5

ROW 55 — 2 brown, 1 gold No. 5

ROW 56 — 2 brown, 1 gold No. 5

ROW 57 — 2 brown, 1 taupe

ROW 58 — 1 brown, 2 taupe

ROW 59 — 1 green No. 1, 2 taupe

ROW 60 — 2 green No. 1, 1 taupe

ROW 61 — 3 green No. 1

ROW 62 — 2 green No. 1, 1 green No. 2

ROW 63 — 1 green No. 1, 2 green No. 2

ROW 64 — 1 green No. 1, 1 green No. 2, 1 green No. 3

ROW 65 — 2 green No. 2, 1 green No. 3

ROW 66 — 1 green No. 2, 2 green No. 3

ROWS 67-68 — 3 green No. 3

AUTUMN SUNSHINE

Oval, 24 x 40 inches, this little rug is completely butted right from
the first two rows. It shows, through its change of color, how you can
enlarge this rug to whatever size you wish by having wider bands
of the color combinations. It has been used many times to show

shades which may be used in a rug to blend well with maple or pine, and it can be made a continuous rug by carrying tweedy mixtures of the tan and brown combinations throughout the rug. Remember that the more rows you have exactly alike or nearly alike, the easier it is to keep the eyes from focusing on the place you change color.

Center is 16 inches long.

ROW 1 — 1 weak rust, 1 med. rust, 1 tweedy mix. overdyed with gold

ROW 2 — 1 gold, 1 med. rust, 1 tweedy mix., overdyed with gold

ROW 3 — 1 spice brown mix., 1 bronze green mix., 1 mahogany

ROW 4 — 1 spice brown, 1 bronze green, 1 olive green

ROWS 5-6 — 1 rust, 1 mummy brown, 1 olive green

ROWS 7-9 — 1 rust, 1 bronze green, 1 khaki into olive green

ROWS 10-11 — 1 golden brown mix., 1 gold tweedy mix., 1 brown

ROW 12 — 1 tan, 1 lt. rust, 1 brown

ROW 13 — 1 med. rust, 1 brown, 1 gold tweedy mix.

ROW 14 — 1 med. rust, 1 brown, 1 old gold

ROW 15 — 1 tan, 1 brown, 1 bronze green mix.

ROW 16 — 1 brown and rust tweed mix., 1 bronze green mix., 1 olive green

ROW 17 — 1 brown and rust tweed mix., 2 olive green

This pattern was worked out with an 8 x 10 ft. rug, with the center 24 inches long. Much tan and many tweeds of beige, brown and rust formed the background, against which the rusts and greens were accented in designs, like light and dark shadows with sunshine flickering over the whole rug, effected through the use of gold dye used over many of the tweed mixtures. Earth colors and greens are always a restful background for such a floor covering.

AUTUMN WINDS

Rectangle, 30 x 48 inches, with a hooked center of autumn-colored leaves strewn on a background which looks windswept. Here and there, metallic gold threads gleam like bright October sunshine. Around the outer border of the three-toned beige and dirt-colored background (beige dyed unevenly in seal brown) is a narrow border of pale green and beige mixture which is used with the two shades of beige to make up the first braid. The first braid is sewn to the tape and is butted as are all other rows.

There are nine braids attached to the center to enlarge it. As spot-dyeing was used for some of the leaves, this same method was used for most of the strips to give the appearance of the same colored bits of scattered leaves throughout the whole rug. The spot-dyeing was done over pale yellow. Even the pale purples of the side motifs are caught in the spot-dyes when the aqua and the crimson come together as the cloth is steaming. The general effect is one of rich fall shades.

The colors in the bands of braid are worked out from the pale yellow and green to the golds, old gold, rusty browns into mulberry, olive greens and rich red brown.

BETSY ROSS

Butted oval, 36" x 50", 14 inch center, 5 shades of cherry red, 5 shades of blue, 3 shades of beige.

ROWS 1-2 — 1 red, 1 med. blue, 1 dark blue
ROW 3 — 1 lt. blue, 1 red, 1 beige
ROW 4 — 1 med. blue, 1 lt. blue, 1 beige
ROWS 5-7 — 2 med. blue, 1 beige, forming diagonals (same colors against each other in successive rows)
ROWS 8-10 — 1 med. blue, 1 beige, 1 red
ROWS 11-13 — 1 med. blue, 1 red, 1 dark blue (keep blues together —diamonds)
ROW 14 — 2 med. blue, 1 red
ROW 15 — 2 med. blue, 1 beige
ROW 16 — 1 med. blue, 1 beige, 1 red
ROW 17 — 1 beige, 2 red (reds against reds for diagonals)
ROW 18 — 3 reds
ROWS 19-20 — 2 red, 1 beige (reds against reds for diagonals)
ROW 21 — 1 red, 1 beige, 1 med. blue
ROWS 22-23 — 1 beige, 2 med. blue (keep blues against blues for diagonals)

ROWS 24-26 — 1 med. blue, 1 red, 1 skipper blue
ROW 27 — 2 skipper blue, 1 navy blue

BLOCK AND ROSETTE (See illustration)

Small rectangle with 5 strand braids combined with 3 strand braids. Center is made of 11 straight braids 28 inches long. Each strand consists of 1 blue, 1 rose, 1 light gray, 1 medium gray and 1 black. These are bound by a 1" wide strip of the black material, then 2 rows of the black are butted around the rug, square corners being turned in the braids. The next 3 rows are made up of 2 rose and 1 black, put together to form rosette-like designs. A solid row of black completes this little mat. The black strands are made of 3 braids.

To make 5-strand braids, number them in your mind from left to right as 1, 2, 3, 4, 5, as they are strung on a large safety pin.

Put 1 over 2 under 3 over 4 under 5. Now with the new order of colors numbered 1, 2, 3, 4, 5, start with the color at your furthest left and put 1 over 2 under 3 over 4 under 5. After awhile you will find that you can braid very easily and fast with both hands. This braiding is what your young son is doing when he braids those leather belts in manual training, but he doesn't have to turn in any raw edges. You must baste yours all out of sight before you start to braid, so you will be braiding with long tubes, or use braid aids.

If you put two strongly contrasting colors beside each other, you will achieve interesting block effect. Checks or tweeds also give intriguing geometric designs, and you can use any number of strands in your braids.

BLUE DIAMONDS (See illustration)

32 x 56 rectangle, corners squared as you lace, 24 inch center, continuous braid.

Center — 6 double rows, 1 tan and white check, 2 gray and blue tweedy mixture.

ROWS 7-8 — 1 medium blue, 2 gray and blue mix
ROW 9 — This row starts the diamond in navy. 4 rows complete it.

Place colors as directed in instructions for design. 1 navy blue,
2 gray and blue mix

ROWS 10-11 — 2 navy blue, 1 gray and blue mix

ROW 12 — 1 navy, 1 gray and blue mix, 1 blue and beige mix

ROWS 13-14 — 1 medium blue, 1 gray, 1 blue and beige mix

ROWS 15-16 — 1 gray, 1 blue and beige mix, 1 brown and gold mix

ROWS 17-18 — 1 medium blue, 1 gray, 1 brown and gold mix

ROW 19 — start of another diamond—1 navy blue, 1 blue gray, 1
beige and gray mix

ROWS 20-21 — 2 navy, 1 gray and beige mix

ROW 22 — 1 navy, 1 blue gray, 1 gray and beige mix

ROW 23 — 1 medium blue, 1 blue gray, 1 gray and beige mix

ROWS 24-25 — 2 medium blue, 1 brown and beige mix

BOUQUET OF ZINNIAS (See illustration)

Clover leaf type rug with 3 15½ inch circles, attached to each other
with a few strong stitches, then the center is filled with butted strips
of braid. It takes two on each side and a very small piece of braid
for the remaining center. If you prefer, you can sew on a piece of
burlap to the wrong side and hook in the background color. Use
gold and brown mixture with green and brown for the center of the
flowers, band with several rows of shaded crimson, put together with
field green, and finish with a few rows of greens, tans and browns.

CALIFORNIA RANCHO

This rug is 10 ft. by 13 ft. and is a continuous braid in the "Hit-or-
Miss" type brought up to date by using one strip of tan and one of
brown with the third strip made up of many shades of reds, golds
and greens. Three breaks are made to emphasize hunter green, and
these green bands make the rug outstanding. The rug was made by
Mildred Murphy of Van Nuys, California, and is pictured in her
family room. Mildred Sprout, a well-known teacher of both hooked
and braided rugs in the Los Angeles area, was the instructor. Mrs.
Sprout says it is very difficult to find many on the West Coast who
will make the fine braids which are so typical of the East Coast,

notably New England. Practically all the rugs are continuous braid, though she does teach Method 7, so that the last rows can be butted.

The center is 3 ft. long and the green bands are used at spaced intervals. When the rug measures approximately 3½ ft. across, double band; 7½ ft., four bands; and the last five rows, for the final band. There are also brown and tan in these green bands, as in all the others.

CHRISTMAS BELLS

9 x 12 butted rug, made mostly with tweeds, checks and mixtures, blues shading from medium-grayed blue to dark blue (lighter than navy), 4 shades of greens, gold and old gold, rich crimson.

Center: 3 ft.

ROWS 1-6 — 1 tan, 1 brown and beige tweed, 1 light green
ROWS 7-10 — 1 tan and gray check, 1 brown and beige check, 1 lt. green
ROWS 11-13 — 1 tan and gray check, 1 red, 1 lt. green (red jewels)
ROW 14 — 1 tan and gray check, 1 lt. green, 1 hunter green
ROWS 15-16 — 1 tan and gray check, 2 hunter green (green diamonds)
ROW 17 — 2 tan and gray check, 1 hunter green
ROW 18 — 2 tan and brown check, 1 tan tweed
ROW 19 — 1 tan and brown check, 2 tan tweed
ROWS 20-23 — 2 tan and brown check, 1 beige and brown mix.
ROWS 24-26 — 1 tan and brown check, 1 tan check, 1 gold
ROWS 27-28 — 1 tan and gray mix., 1 gray tweed, 1 medium blue
ROW 29 — 2 medium blue, 1 gray tweed (forming blue ric-rac)
ROWS 30-34 — 1 blue (second shade), 2 gray tweed
ROW 35 — 3 blues (1 shade No. 2, 2 shades No. 3)
ROWS 36-37 — 1 blue and gray mixture, 2 tan tweed
ROWS 38-40 — 1 old gold, 1 tan tweed, 1 gray and tan tweed
ROWS 41-44 — 1 golden brown, 1 tan tweed, 1 gray and tan tweed
ROW 45 — 1 green tweed, 1 tan tweed, 1 gray and tan tweed
ROWS 46-47 — 1 green tweed, 1 tan tweed, 1 light brown
ROWS 48-49 — 1 green tweed, 1 dark green, 1 brown and beige tweed

ROWS 50-52 — 2 dark green, 1 beige tweed (double green diamonds)

ROW 53 — 1 dark green, 1 green tweed, 1 light tan

ROWS 54-55 — 1 tan tweed, 1 green tweed, 1 gray tweed

ROW 56 — 1 red, 1 gray tweed, 1 green tweed

ROWS 57-59 — 1 red, 1 gray tweed, 1 beige tweed (red jewels)

ROWS 60-62 — 1 green tweed, 1 gray tweed, 1 beige mix.

ROWS 63-65 — 2 beige mix., 1 brown and beige mix.

ROWS 66-67 — 3 tan and brown mix.

ROWS 68-70 — 2 tan and brown mix., 1 gray and blue mix.

ROWS 71-73 — 1 tan and brown mix., 2 gray and blue mix.

ROW 74 — 2 tan and brown mix., 1 medium blue

ROW 75 — 1 tan and brown mix., 2 medium blue (blue ric-rac)

ROW 76 — 1 tan and brown mix., 1 medium blue, 1 blue-gray mix.

ROW 77 — 1 medium blue, 2 brown and gray mix.

ROW 78 — 1 blue No. 1, 1 blue and gray mix., 1 blue No. 2

ROW 79 — 2 blue No. 2, 1 blue and gray mix.

ROW 80 — 2 blue No. 2, 1 blue No. 3 (arrowhead)

ROW 81 — 3 blue No. 3

CIGARETTE MONEY (See illustration)

Mary Beach of Woodbridge, Conn., gave up cigarettes and put her extra money into materials for this rug. Except for two camel's-hair coats and two discarded army blankets, the rest of the cloth was purchased from her "cigarette money." Hence the name.

The rug is 7 x 10 and is used with some beautiful antiques—chests, table and chairs are gleaming mahogany. The rug has a subdued background and the few colors are introduced subtly so that none overshadows the other. The rich brocade of the red draperies with their narrow silver and gold stripes pick up the deep reds in the rug.

Mrs. Beach made her rug for under $50, though she assures everyone all of the money did not come from unbought cigarettes. In the doorways are two small rugs which blend with the large one and tie in with orientals in the rest of the house.

ROWS 1-4 — 1 red, 1 beige, 1 tan tweed

ROWS 5-6 — 1 red, 2 tan tweed

ROW 7 — 1 khaki drab, 1 tan tweed, 1 gray tweed

ROWS 8-9 — 2 khaki drab, 1 gray tweed

ROWS 10-11 — 1 khaki drab, 1 gray tweed, 1 tan

ROWS 12-13 — 1 khaki drab, 1 red, 1 tan

ROWS 14-15 — 1 khaki drab, 1 gold, 1 tan

ROWS 16-17 — 2 khaki drab, 1 gold

ROW 18 — 3 khaki drab

ROWS 19-20 — 2 khaki drab, 1 green

ROWS 21-23 — 1 khaki drab, 1 red and black check, 1 beige and brown tweed

ROWS 24-25 — 1 khaki drab, 1 tan, 1 black and white tweed

ROWS 26-27 — 2 tans, 1 black and white check tweed

ROW 28 — 1 red, 1 tan, 1 khaki drab

ROW 29 — 2 red, 1 khaki

ROW 30 — 1 red, 1 khaki, 1 tan

ROWS 31-33 — 1 tan, 1 khaki, 1 gray tweed

ROW 34 — 2 tan, 1 gray tweed

ROWS 35-36 — 1 tan, 1 gray tweed, 1 khaki

ROWS 37-39 — 1 tan, 1 gold, 1 beige mix.

ROW 40 — 1 tan, 1 red, 1 beige mix.

ROWS 41-43 — 2 tan, 1 khaki

ROWS 44-45 — 1 gold, 1 tan, 1 beige check

ROW 46 — 2 gold, 1 beige check

ROW 47 — 1 gold, 1 beige check, 1 tan

ROW 48 — 1 khaki, 1 beige check, 1 green tweed

ROW 49 — 1 khaki, 1 green, 1 beige check

ROW 50 — 1 khaki, 1 green, 1 gray

ROW 51 — 1 brown and beige check, 1 red, 1 gray

ROW 52 — 1 gold, 1 beige, 1 khaki

ROWS 53-54 — 1 gold, 1 old gold, 1 beige

ROWS 55-56 — 1 gray, 2 beige mix.

ROW 57 — 1 gray, 1 beige mix., 1 green

ROWS 58-59 — 2 gray, 1 beige

ROWS 60-61 — 1 gray, 1 beige, 1 green

ROWS 62-63 — 1 gray, 1 beige mix., 1 tan

ROWS 64-65 — 1 old gold, 1 beige mix., 1 tan

ROW 66 — 1 beige mix., 1 gray, 1 red check

ROW 67 — 1 gray, 2 red
ROW 68 — 1 gray, 1 red, 1 green

CONTENTMENT

Three-circle rug, 6 x 9, butted. 3 centers are 12 inches in diameter. 45 rows are attached to the three circles after they have been joined with a few strong stitches. Four shades of blue and four shades of rose are used with beige and beige tweedy mixtures.

Two end circles are made of blue No. 1 (light) and blue No. 2 shades with 1 strand of beige tweed. Center circle is made of rose No. 1 and rose No. 2 with 1 beige tweed.

ROW 1 — 2 beige tweed, 1 rose No. 2
ROW 2 — 2 beige tweed, 1 blue No. 1
ROWS 3-4 — 1 beige tweed, 1 blue No. 1, 1 blue No. 2
ROW 5 — 1 beige tweed, 1 blue No. 2, 1 rose No. 1
ROWS 6-7 — 1 beige tweed, 1 rose No. 2, 1 rose No. 1
ROWS 8-10 — 1 beige tweed, 2 rose No. 2
ROWS 11-12 — 1 beige tweed, 1 rose No. 2, 1 blue No. 2
ROW 13 — 3 blue No. 2
ROWS 14-16 — 1 beige mix., 2 blue No. 2
ROW 17 — 2 beige mix., 1 blue No. 2
ROWS 18-20 — 2 beige mix., 1 rose No. 2
ROWS 21-24 — 1 beige mix., 2 rose No. 2
ROWS 25-27 — 2 beige mix., 1 blue No. 2
ROWS 28-30 — 1 beige, 1 blue No. 2, 1 blue No. 3
ROW 31 — 1 beige mix., 2 blue No. 3
ROW 32 — 3 blue No. 3
ROWS 33-35 — 1 beige mix., 2 blue No. 2
ROWS 36-37 — 1 beige mix., 1 blue No. 2, 1 blue No. 1
ROWS 38-39 — 1 beige mix., 1 blue No. 2, 1 rose No. 2
ROWS 40-41 — 1 beige mix., 1 rose No. 3, 1 rose No. 4
ROW 42 — 1 beige mix., 1 rose No. 4, 1 blue No. 4
ROWS 43-45 — 1 beige mix., 2 blue No. 4

This lovely rug was made by Ruth Billington, Attleboro, Mass., and was her first attempt at braiding.

COUNTRY KITCHEN (See illustration)

My own rug, "COUNTRY KITCHEN," is made of only three colors, the ones most commonly used among the country people of one hundred years ago. It is a butted rug, 32½ x 56½ inches, with 2 ft. center. Material required—4 lbs. black, 3 lbs. red, 1½ lbs. gray tweedy mixture. Any three colors may be combined in this rug pattern if they contrast well. It is a good basic pattern to learn design, amount of materials used, and the setting up of a pattern. The size will please anyone. Center has 5 double rows, 1 red, 1 black, 1 gray mixture. Keep like colors against each other throughout the rug as you lace.

ROW 6 — 2 red, 1 black
ROW 7 — 3 red
ROW 8 — 3 black
ROWS 9-10 — 1 red, 2 black
ROW 11 — 2 red, 1 black
ROWS 12-15 — 1 red, 1 black, 1 gray mixture
ROWS 16-17 — 2 red, 1 black
ROWS 18-19 — 1 red, 2 black
ROW 20 — 2 red, 1 black
ROW 21 — 1 red, 2 black
ROW 22 — 3 black

DOMINO

Rug made by Lillian Grady, Quincy, Mass., Marie Bond of West Roxbury, teacher and designer of rug.

36 inch square mat, squared with sharp turns in the braid, continuous braid. Study in black and white. Squared from the start, with last row butted.

ROWS 1-4 — 2 white, 1 gray No. 2 shade (whites together as you lace)
ROW 5 — 1 white, 2 gray No. 2 shade
ROWS 6-7 — 1 gray No. 1, 2 gray and white tweedy mixture (tweeds together as you lace for diagonals)
ROW 8 — 1 gray No. 1, 1 gray and white tweedy mixture, 1 charcoal and gray mix

ROWS 9-10 — 1 gray No. 1, 2 charcoal and gray mix. (same colors against each other when lacing)

ROW 11 — 1 gray No. 1, 1 charcoal and gray mix., 1 gray and white tweedy mixture

ROWS 12-15 — 1 gray No. 2 shade, 1 white, 1 charcoal and gray mix.

ROWS 16-17 — 1 gray No. 2 shade, 1 white and light gray mix., 1 charcoal mix.

ROW 18 — 1 gray and white tweed, 2 black and white tweed

ROW 19 — 2 gray and white tweed, 1 black and white tweed (keep same colors against each other when lacing)

ROW 20 — 1 gray and white tweed, 2 black and white tweed

ROW 21 — 2 gray and white tweed, 1 black and white tweed

ROW 22 — 1 gray and white tweed, 2 black and white tweed

ROWS 23-25 — 1 bluish gray and white tweed, 1 black and white tweed

ROW 26 — 2 gray and white tweed, 1 black and white tweedy mixture (tapered end)

ROW 27 — 3 black and white tweedy mixture (butted)

Because all of these grays had a bluish cast and because many blacks have the same bluish tone, the rug has a bluish overtone, though the shadings are beautifully blended from the whites through the deepest grays into black.

FAMILY TREASURE (See illustration)

42 x 66—24 inch center oval rug, continuous flat braids, ½″ wide.

ROWS 1-5 Half of center — 1 medium brown mixture, 1 medium blue, 1 navy and white check

ROWS 6-7 — 1 medium brown mix, 1 blue mix, 1 gray

ROWS 8-9 — 1 medium brown mix, 1 blue mix, 1 beige

ROWS 10-12 — 1 medium brown mix, 1 blue mix, 1 coral

ROW 13 — 1 gray, 1 coral, 1 brown and gold mix

ROWS 14-15 — 1 gray mix, 1 brown and gold mix, 1 dark blue

ROWS 16-18 — 1 gray mix, 1 brown and gold mix, 1 navy and white check

ROWS 19-22 — 1 medium green, 1 blue and white check, 1 tan and gold mix

ROWS 23-24 — 1 beige, 1 gray mix, 1 tan and gold mix

ROWS 25-26 — 1 coral, 1 gray mix, 1 tan and gold mix

ROW 27 — 1 navy mix, 1 gray mix, 1 light brown and gold mix

ROWS 28-30 — 1 navy and white check, 1 green, 1 brown and gold mix

FIRELIGHT

This rug is a lovely combination of rose and green shades and is so blended that it can be made with a continuous braid or butted. Much checked material was used in both pink and gray, with black used as an accent.

There are many fine rug braiders in the southeastern part of Massachusetts and the nearby Providence area. Ursula Ross of Norwood, R.I., who made this rug and many other fine ones, is a meticulous worker with a keen eye for color.

8 x 10 oval 2 ft. center. Keep same colors against each other when lacing. Make center 3 ft. long for 9 x 12.

ROWS 1-9 — pink check, 1 gray check, 1 pink

ROW 10 — pink check, 1 dusty pink, 1 pink

ROW 11 — pink check, 1 dusty pink, 1 rose

ROW 12 — pink check, 1 maroon, 1 rose

ROW 13 — 1 wine, 1 maroon, 1 rose

ROW 14 — 1 wine, 1 maroon, 1 pink check

ROW 15 — gray check, 1 maroon, 1 pink check

ROW 16 — gray check, 2 pink check

ROW 17 — gray check, 1 med. gray, 1 pink check

ROW 18 — gray check, 1 black, 1 pink check

ROW 19 — gray check, 1 dark green, 1 pink check

ROW 20 — gray check, 1 dark green, 1 light green

ROW 21 — 1 dark green, 2 light green

ROW 22 — 2 dark green, 1 light green

ROW 23 — 1 dark green, 2 light green

ROW 24 — pink check, 1 dark green, 1 light green

ROW 25 — pink check, 1 light green, 1 black

ROW 26 — pink check, 1 light green, 1 medium gray
ROW 27 — 2 medium gray, 1 pink check
ROW 28 — pink check, 1 gray check, 1 med. gray
ROW 29 — 2 pink check, 1 gray check
ROW 30 — 2 pink check, 1 pink
ROW 31 — 2 pink check, 1 dusty pink
ROW 32 — pink check, 1 dusty pink, 1 rose
ROW 33 — pink check, 1 rose, 1 maroon
ROW 34 — wine, 1 rose, maroon
ROW 35 — wine, 1 pink check, 1 rose
ROW 36 — 2 pink check, 1 rose
ROW 37 — 2 pink check, 1 gray check
ROW 38 — pink check, 2 gray check
ROW 39 — black, 2 gray check
ROW 40 — 2 black, 1 gray check
ROW 41 — black, 2 gray check
ROW 42 — pink check, 2 gray check
ROW 43 — pink check, gray check, 1 light green
ROW 44 — pink check, 2 light green
ROWS 45-46 — pink check, 1 dark green, 1 light green
ROWS 47-48 — 2 pink check, 1 dark green
ROWS 49-56 — pink check, 1 dark green, 1 wine

FISHER BOY

"FISHER BOY" was originally a 15-inch hooked chair-seat, but has been enlarged to a mat by adding 8 narrow braids which pick up the greens of the grass, the faded straw colors in the wide-brimmed straw hat and the trousers, and the deeper tones of the khaki. A fleck of red in some of the tan mixtures repeats the red of the jacket.

When one sees this little fisherman, Whittier's poem "The Barefoot Boy" immediately comes to mind, and one can almost hear that "merry whistled tune" from under the wide-brimmed hat as he trudges jauntily through the field dotted here and there with gay flowers, while the tiny speckled brook trout dangles from the end of his pole.

All four of my grandsons are avid fishermen, so it looks as if I must make repeats of the little mat.

The fine hooking was done by Margaret Russell of Waterbury, Conn., an expert hooking teacher, who put in many of the little details not on the original pattern.

As in all rugs with hooked centers, the first row was sewn to the tape with all other rows butted, the joinings being spaced around the mat which is now a 25 in. round rug.

Reseda green dye was used in three shades, old gold over gray and over a light tan mixture, and medium brown over a gray mix. These gave tones which pulled out the size of the rug without detracting from the pattern of the center.

ROW 1 — reseda green over gray, reseda green over beige, gold over gray mix

ROW 2 — reseda green over gray 2nd shade, gold over gray mix

ROW 3 — reseda green over gray 2nd shade, old gold over tan, gold over gray

ROW 4 — reseda green over gray 2nd shade, old gold over tan, 1 tan flecked tweed

ROW 5 — reseda green over gray 2nd shade, old gold over tan, 1 med. brown mix

ROW 6 — reseda green over gray 2nd shade, 1 tan, 1 med. brown mix

ROW 7 — reseda green over gray 2nd shade, 1 old gold over tan, 1 med. brown mix

ROW 8 — reseda green over gray 2nd shade, 1 reseda green 3rd shade, 1 med. brown mix

FOOTSTEPS

Stair-treads may be oval or square-cornered and can be continuous braids, for as a rule, they are made out of short ends. You can always have a little design by making an arrowhead on the last two rows as I have done with the rectangles. In all these treads, a dull red, gray or beige mixtures (strong tweeds), a grayed soft turquoise blue, and navy are used. All the designs are different, some of the treads having been started with the blues and others with reds. Myrtle green was dyed over some of the gray mixtures to obtain a weak blue-green.

These colors are used to blend in with the large Persian rug at the foot of the stairs. The treads measure 10 in. by 29 in. and were started with 19 in. centers.

For treads, make a paper pattern of the size you want as a tread, and measure length and width, whether you are making ovals or rectangles. The difference between the length and the width will be the length of the center before you make that first bend. If you are a tight braider, allow an extra inch.

If you have lots of odds and ends you would like to use up, make your treads with one strand each of brown, black, navy blue, brown or even a maroon, one strand of mixtures, and the third one of short ends. A variation of this could be two mixtures and the third one of colors. Or you could use one black, one mixture and the third strand of all colors. Or you might like to use two strands of color with one black. I do like tweeds in treads for they do not show soil as fast as the solid colors do. Be sure that all your materials are firmly woven and a good weight to stand up under constant wear in the same spots. Lace as you braid, so that your adjacent colors will harmonize.

Treads are economical and easy to make, can be replaced one at a time, and with rubber rug-lining under each, they do not necessitate any tacking to the stairs.

THE GLAD WELCOME (See illustration)

Hall runner 27″ x 77″. Center made of 14 straight braids (7 matching pairs) 48″ long, laced together with ends butted to the next row which goes all around as do the rest of the braids. Care must be used to work from the center out, in order to keep the design balanced. Put strands of color on your safety pin in just the opposite order for the second side or all design will be lost. Check this order at the beginning of each row for the second side. This will also keep the ends even. After the center is made, all other rows are butted! A stair runner is made in the same way except that the center is wider and border consists of only 2 or 3 rows.

ROW 1 — 2 black, 1 blue (form black diamond with first row of each half)
ROW 2 — 1 black, 2 blue (start of blue diamond)

ROW 3 — 2 blue, 1 beige tweedy mixture

ROW 4 — 1 blue, 1 beige mix, 1 rose red (raspberry or garnet red)

ROW 5 — 1 beige, 2 red (now starting to form diamond in red)

ROW 6 — 1 beige, 2 red

ROW 7 — 1 beige, 1 red, 1 olive green

ROW 8 — This is the first row to go all around. 1 green and yellow plaid, 1 field green, 1 beige mix

ROW 9 — 1 green and yellow plaid, 2 field green

ROW 10 — 1 field green, 1 green and yellow plaid, 1 gold and black check

ROW 11 — 2 green and yellow plaid, 1 gold and black check

ROW 12 — 1 green and yellow plaid, 1 gold and black check

ROWS 13-14 — 1 yellow and black check, 2 medium blue, put blues together

ROW 15 — 1 gray mix, 1 medium brown, 1 field green

ROW 16 — 1 gray mix, 1 field green, 1 rose red

ROW 17 — 1 gray mix, 2 rose red

ROW 18 — 1 black, 1 medium blue mix, 1 rose red

ROW 19 — 1 black, 2 blue mix

ROW 20 — 2 black, 1 medium blue mix

GODEY SPRAY

Rectangular hooked center, about 18 x 30, with 10 rows of braid. Corners are squared in the braid, and are butted, the first one being sewn to the tape, while the others are laced. Design is of large, graceful sprays hooked in blue greens with a two tone camel hair color background. The berries are shades of red. Two old polo coats were used for the background and for the braids, running in every strand. The first two strands are of the tan with tan mixtures, then the blue greens are added for 6 rows. The last two rows have the tan, and the darkest shades of the blue and field greens are used.

GOLDEN GLOW

"GOLDEN GLOW" is a 3-circle rug, clover leaf type.

The three pale yellow, pale gold, and beige centers are 5½ in. circles which are tapered off. The rest of the rug is butted. The

12 inch circles shade out to gold and tan. When I had completed them and sewn them into place, I cut two pieces of burlap to fit the center hole. I hooked each one of these pieces in the tans of the last rows of the circles. On one side, I put in my initials and the date. Unfortunately, the picture was taken of the wrong side—I forgot to have the rug changed to the right side to show the marking. It is a simple trick to hook in your own initials, much easier than braiding them. Use one of the deeper tans against the light beige.

For the outer rows, old gold was dyed over beige in two shades —over gray for a dulled chartreuse shade, tans, golden and medium browns; bronze-green, olive green and marine green were used with three shades of rust.

If this rug were to be continued, it would eventually become round once more. The indentations lose their sharp turns as the rug grows larger, and the sharp square corners and then the modified square corners are used in these places instead of squeezing in the braids.

ROWS 1-3 — pale yellow, pale gold, beige (taper off)
ROW 4 — pale yellow, pale gold, beige
ROWS 5-6 — deeper yellow, tan, beige
ROW 7 — deeper yellow, 2 tan
ROW 8 — deeper yellow, 1 tan, chartreuse (gold over gray)
ROW 9 — old gold, 1 tan, chartreuse
    Attach circles
ROW 10 — Same as Row 9
ROWS 11-12 — 1 old gold, 2 tan
ROW 13 — 1 old gold, 1 tan, 1 golden brown
ROWS 14-15 — 1 bronze, 1 golden brown, 1 rust No. 1 shade
ROW 16 — 1 bronze 2nd shade, 1 golden brown, 1 pale rust
ROW 17 — 1 bronze 3rd shade, 1 golden brown, 1 2nd shade rust
ROW 18 — 1 olive, 2 marine green
ROW 19 — 1 bronze green, 1 rust 2nd shade, 1 golden brown
ROW 20 — 1 bronze green, 1 rust 2nd shade, 1 gold over gray
ROW 21 — 1 bronze green 2nd shade, 1 rust 3rd shade, 1 gold over gray
ROW 22 — 1 bronze green 2nd shade, 1 rust 3rd shade, 1 golden brown

ROWS 23-24 — 1 olive green, 1 rust 3rd shade, 1 medium brown
ROW 25 — 2 olive green, 1 rust 3rd shade
ROW 26 — 1 olive green, 2 marine green

GOLDEN LATTICE

This is a 3 x 5 rectangle, continuous braid, squared as you lace, monochromatic rug, worked out in a diagonal weave, in shades of yellows, which deepen into golds, rusts, tans, and browns, with tans or tan tweeds carried through the whole rug. The diagonal weave is achieved by keeping the same colors against each other in adjacent rows, as you lace.

Because so many yellows and golds are used, the rug seems to be full of little yellow and gold butterflies.

Needed for this rug are 3 lbs. yellows and golds, 3 lbs. of tans and tan tweeds, 1 lb. of rust tweed and 2 lbs. of browns.

Center — 2 ft.
ROWS 1-5 — 1 yellow, 2 tan
ROWS 6-7 — 1 yellow, 1 tan, 1 golden brown
ROWS 8-11 — 1 gold check, 1 tan, 1 golden brown
ROWS 12-14 — 1 gold check, 1 tan tweed, 1 golden brown
ROWS 15-18 — 1 gold tweed, 1 tan tweed, 1 pale rust
ROWS 19-20 — 1 gold tweed, 1 tan, 1 light brown
ROWS 21-22 — 1 gold and rust check, 1 tan, 1 light brown
ROWS 23-25 — 1 tan and rust check, 1 tan, 1 brown
ROWS 26-27 — 1 tan tweed, 1 tan, 1 brown

HARMONY

3 x 5 ft. oval rug made by Marie Bond, West Roxbury, teacher in the Boston, Mass., area. Continuous braid except for the last row which is butted.

2 ft. center: 4 shades of rust dyed over pink; 4 shades myrtle green over light blue.

Center—diagonal weave—keep same colors together when lacing.

ROWS 1-3 — 2 beige, 1 brown tweed
ROW 4 — 1 beige, 2 brown tweed

ROW 5 — 2 tweed, 1 brown (keep tweeds against tweeds when lacing)

ROW 6 — 1 tweed, 2 brown (brown arrow)

ROW 7 — 2 brown, 1st shade of green (browns against brown)

ROW 8 — 1 brown, 1st shade of green, 2nd shade of green

ROW 9 — 1 brown, 2nd shade of green, 3rd shade of green

ROW 10 — 1 brown, 3rd shade of green, 4th shade of green

ROW 11 — 1 brown, 4th shade of green, 1 beige

ROW 12 — 2 brown, 1 beige (keep same colors together when lacing)

ROW 13 — 1 brown, 2 beige (keep same colors together when lacing—arrow)

ROW 14 — 2 beige, 1st shade of rust

ROW 15 — 1 beige, 1st shade of rust, 1 tweed

ROW 16 — 1st shade rust, 2nd shade rust, 1 tweed

ROW 17 — 2nd shade rust, 3rd shade rust, 1 tweed

ROW 18 — 3rd shade rust, 4th shade rust, 1 tweed

ROW 19 — 4th shade rust, 1 brown, 1 tweed

ROW 20 — 4th shade rust, 2 brown

ROW 21 — 1st shade green, 2 brown

ROW 22 — 1st shade green, 1 brown, 2nd shade green

ROW 23 — 2nd shade green, 1 brown, 2nd shade green

ROW 24 — 3rd shade green, 1 brown, 4th shade green

ROW 25 — 4th shade green, 1 brown, 1 beige

ROW 26 — 2 beige, 1 brown (keep same colors together when lacing)

ROW 27 — 1 beige, 2 brown (taper for rat tail finish)

ROWS 28-29 — 3 brown (butted row)

HAPPY HOURS (See illustration)

Mrs. Harold Hogarth of Wrentham, Mass., made this long narrow
rectangular rug for her television room. The rug measures 7 x 13 and
is squared in the braid with the sharp square turns. A tweed of beige
and brown with flecks of gold, red and green runs almost throughout every row. Three shades of rose-reds are used with three shades
of olive and hunter greens, tan, golden, spice and dark browns.

The rug has a 6 ft. center.

ROWS 1-6 — 1 beige and brown tweed, 1 medium brown, 1 old gold

ROWS 7-9 — 1 beige and brown tweed, 1 hunter green, 1 old gold

ROWS 10-11 — 1 beige and brown tweed, 2 hunter green (greens together when lacing to form green diamonds)

ROW 12 — 1 beige and brown tweed, 1 old rose shade No. 1, 1 green

ROWS 13-14 — 1 beige and brown tweed, 1 old rose shade No. 1, taupe

ROWS 15-17 — 1 beige and brown tweed, 1 taupe, 1 medium brown

ROWS 18-22 — 1 beige and brown tweed, 1 medium green, 1 medium brown

ROWS 23-26 — 1 beige and brown tweed, 1 old gold, 1 deeper brown

ROWS 27-28 — 1 beige and brown tweed, 1 brown No. 2, 1 old rose No. 2

ROW 29 — 1 beige and brown tweed, 1 green, 1 old rose No. 2

ROWS 30-31 — 1 green No. 2 shade, 2 rose No. 2

ROWS 32-33 — 2 green No. 2 shade, 1 rose No. 2 (greens together when lacing)

ROWS 34-36 — 1 green No. 2 shade, 1 rose No. 3, 1 beige and brown tweed

ROW 37 — 1 green No. 2 shade, 1 taupe, 1 beige and brown tweed

ROW 38 — 1 green shade No. 3, 1 taupe, 1 beige and brown tweed

ROWS 39-40 — 2 green shade No. 3, 1 beige and brown tweed (greens together when lacing)

ROW 41 — 1 green shade No. 3, 1 beige and brown tweed, 1 taupe

ROW 42 — 1 old gold, 1 taupe, 1 beige and brown tweed

ROW 43 — 1 brown, 1 taupe, 1 beige and brown tweed

ROW 44 — 1 brown, 1 bronze green, 1 beige and brown tweed

ROW 45 — 2 olive green, 1 beige and brown tweed (greens together when lacing)

ROW 46 — 1 olive green, 1 garnet, 1 beige and brown tweed

ROWS 47-48 — 2 garnet, 1 beige and brown tweed (reds together when lacing for diamond)

ROW 49 — 1 deep red, 1 taupe, 1 beige and brown tweed mixture

ROW 50 — 1 brown, 1 taupe, 1 beige and brown tweed mixture

ROWS 51-52 — 1 brown, 2 brown tweed

ROWS 53-54 — 2 brown, 1 brown tweed-brown diagonals

ROWS 55-56 — 1 deeper brown, 2 brown tweed

ROWS 57-58 — 1 brown, 1 deeper brown, 1 brown tweed mixture

HEARTHSIDE (See illustration)

Here is a large 12 ft. round rug which brings warmth and cheer to a room with a stone fireplace, pine paneling and maple furniture. Tweeds of brown and white, brown and beige, and green and blue are used as the background and tie all the other colors together. The rug was made by and is pictured in the home of Mrs. Hubert Eva of Sandwich, Ill., with Leila C. Lindahl of Geneva, Ill., teacher. Continuous braid.

ROWS 1-6 — 1 rust, 1 tan, 1 green, brown and white check

ROWS 7-11 — 1 rust, 1 brown rust, 1 green, brown and white check

ROW 12 — olive green, 1 brown rust, green, brown and white check

ROWS 13-16 — 1 olive green, 1 brown rust, 1 brown and white tweed

ROWS 17-19 — 1 green, brown and white check, 1 gray and brown mix, 1 brown and white mix

ROWS 20-21 — 1 gold, 1 green, brown and white check, 1 gray and brown mix

ROW 22 — 1 gold, 1 brown and tan mix, 1 brown and white tweed

ROWS 23-25 — 1 brown rust, 1 brown and tan mix, 1 brown and white tweed

ROWS 26-28 — 1 gold, 1 light blue and green plaid, 1 brown and white tweed

ROW 29 — 1 olive green, 1 grayish tan mix, 1 brown and white tweed

ROW 30 — 1 lt. rust, 1 grayish tan mix, 1 brown and white tweed

ROWS 31-33 — 1 gold, 1 grayish tan mix, 1 brown and white tweed

ROWS 34-35 — 1 green tweed, 1 grayish tan mix, 1 brown and white tweed

ROWS 36-39 — 1 lt. bright green, 1 grayish tan mix, 1 brown and white tweed

ROW 40 — brown and tan tweed, 1 green tweed, 1 brown and white tweed

ROWS 41-43 — 1 lt. rust, 1 golden rust, 1 brown and white tweed

ROWS 44-46 — 1 olive green, 1 lt. brown, 1 brown and white tweed

ROW 47 — 1 green, 1 brown tweed, 1 brown and white tweed

ROWS 48-50 — 1 gold, 1 brown tweed, 1 brown and white tweed check

ROW 51 — 1 bright green, 1 brown tweed, 1 dark brown

ROWS 52-53 — 1 bright green, 1 brown tweed, 1 lt. brown

ROWS 54-55 — 1 lt. rust, 1 brown tweed, 1 lt. brown

ROW 56 — 1 lt. rust, 1 lt. brown, 1 blue and brown tweed

ROW 57-58 — 1 lt. rust, 1 olive green, 1 blue and brown tweed

ROW 59 — 1 gold and brown plaid, 1 olive green, 1 blue and brown tweed

ROWS 60-62 — 2 gold and brown plaid, 1 brown and white tweed

ROW 63 — 1 gold and brown plaid, 1 brown plaid, 1 herringbone tweed

ROWS 64-66 — 1 bright green, 1 brown plaid, 1 herringbone tweed

ROW 67 — 1 olive green, 1 brown rust, 1 herringbone tweed

ROWS 68-70 — 1 bronze green, 1 brown rust, 1 herringbone tweed

ROW 71 — 1 bright green, 1 brown rust, 1 herringbone tweed

ROW 72 — 1 bronze, 1 brown rust, 1 med. brown

ROW 73 — 1 bronze, 1 olive green, 1 brown tweed

ROW 74 — 1 bronze, 1 olive green, 1 blue green

ROWS 75-77 — 1 brown rust, 1 olive green, 1 blue green

HEARTHSIDE COMFORT

9 x 12 continuous or butted rug; 3 ft. center.

ROWS 1-8 — 1 tan and beige tweed, 1 gray mixture, 1 medium blue shade No. 2

ROWS 9-12 — 1 tan and beige tweed, 1 gold and brown check, 1 gray mixture

ROWS 13-15 — 1 tan and beige tweed, 1 gold, 1 gray mixture

ROWS 16-18 — 1 tan and beige tweed, 1 old gold, 1 blue shade No. 1 (start blue diamonds)

ROWS 19-20 — 1 tan and brown tweed, 1 blue shade No. 1, 1 blue shade No. 2

ROWS 21-23 — 1 tan and brown tweed, 1 blue shade No. 2, 1 medium brown

ROWS 24-26 — 1 tan and brown tweed, 1 brown, 1 green mixture

ROWS 27-28 — 1 tan and brown tweed, 2 green mix (greens against each other)

Block and Rosette

Blue Diamonds

Bouquet of Zinnias

Cigarette Money

Country Kitchen

Family Treasure

Glad Welcome

Happy Hours

Hearthside

Memory Lane

Merry-go-round

Patchwork

October Hills

Starlight

Welcome

ROW 29 — 1 tan and brown tweed, 1 green mix, 1 tan (finish green diamonds)

ROWS 30-31 — 1 tan and brown tweed, 1 gold, 1 gray and brown mix

ROWS 32-33 — 1 blue No. 2, 1 gold, 1 gray and brown mix

ROWS 34-35 — 2 blue No. 2, 1 gray and brown mix. (keep blues together)

ROW 36 — 2 blue No. 2, 1 blue No. 3

ROWS 37-38 — 2 blue No. 3, 1 gray mix

ROWS 39-40 — 1 blue No. 3, 1 gray mix., 1 beige mix. (finish blue diamonds)

ROWS 41-43 — 1 tan and brown tweed, 1 gray mix., 1 beige mix.

ROW 44 — 1 tan and brown tweed, 1 reseda green No. 1 shade, 1 beige

ROWS 45-46 — 1 tan and brown tweed, 1 green No. 1, 1 green No. 2 (greens together)

ROW 47 — 2 reseda green No. 2, 1 hunter green and black check

ROWS 48-50 — 2 green and black check, 1 deep rose (use mahogany dye over pink)

ROWS 51-53 — 1 green and black check, 1 rose shade No. 1, 1 shade No. 2 (keep against each other when lacing)

ROW 54 — 2 rose No. 2, 1 rose No. 3

ROWS 55-57 — 2 rose No. 3, 1 beige mixture

ROWS 58-60 — 1 rose No. 3, 1 beige mixture, 1 gray mixture

ROWS 61-63 — 1 beige mix, 1 gold, 1 gray mix.

ROWS 64-66 — 2 beige and brown mix., 1 old gold

ROWS 67-69 — 2 beige and brown mix., 1 gray mix.

ROWS 70-73 — 1 beige and brown mix., 1 gray mix., 1 blue and gray mix.

ROWS 74-75 — 1 blue and gray mix., 1 tan, 1 beige and brown mix.

ROWS 76-77 — 1 tan, 1 brown mix., 1 reseda green No. 3

ROWS 78-79 — 1 brown mix., 2 green No. 3

ROW 80 — 1 brown mix., 1 green No. 3, 1 gray and blue mix

ROW 81 — 2 brown mix., 1 gray and blue mix

HEART'S DESIRE

Made for Mrs. George R. Ingram of Stamford, Conn. 9 x 10½ continuous braided rug made with a background of men's worsteds which range from gray and blue mixtures with green and gray tweeds to the red lines in the tiny checks of the better worsteds. The rug seems to shade out from light beige mixtures through blues, dull reds and greens back to the gray and beige again, yet there is no break in the continuity of the colors. The men's wear has the faculty of pulling all these colors together and blending them into a subtle harmony of shades. None of the material is dyed, but the impression is that much of the fabric came from the same dye pot.

The center is 18 inches long—make 3 ft. for a 9 x 12 ft. rug.

ROWS 1-10 — 1 medium blue, 2 blue and gray mixture
ROWS 11-13 — 1 beige, 2 blue and gray mixture
ROW 14 — 1 beige, 1 blue and gray mixture, 1 medium blue mix.
ROW 15 — 1 beige, 1 blue and gray mixture, 1 maroon
ROWS 16-18 — 1 green mix, 1 gray mix., 1 maroon
ROWS 19-20 — 1 green mix, 2 maroon
ROWS 21-22 — 2 green mix, 1 maroon
ROWS 23-24 — 1 green mix, 1 gray mix., 1 maroon
ROWS 25-27 — 1 beige, 2 gray mix.,
ROWS 28-29 — 2 beige, 1 gray mix.
ROWS 30-33 — 2 gray mix., 1 blue and gray mix.
ROWS 34-36 — 1 gray mix., 1 blue and gray mix., 1 medium blue
ROWS 37-38 — 1 blue, 1 blue and gray mix., 1 beige
ROWS 39-41 — 2 gray mix., 1 green
ROWS 42-45 — 1 gray mix., 1 green, 1 maroon
ROWS 46-48 — 1 gray mix., 1 beige, 1 maroon
ROW 49 — 1 gray mix., 1 blue, 1 blue and gray mix.
ROWS 50-54 — 1 gray mix., 2 blue
ROWS 55-57 — 2 gray mix., 1 blue mix.
ROWS 58-59 — 1 gray mix., 1 blue mix., 1 maroon
ROWS 60-62 — 2 gray mix., 1 maroon
ROWS 63-65 — 1 gray mix., 1 maroon, 1 green
ROWS 66-67 — 1 beige mix., 1 maroon, 1 green
ROW 68 — 2 beige mix., 1 green
ROW 69 — 1 beige, 1 gray mix., 1 med. blue
ROW 70-72 — 1 blue and gray mix, 1 gray mix., 1 blue
ROWS 73-74 — 1 blue and gray mix, 1 gray mix., 1 maroon
ROWS 75-77 — 1 blue and gray mix, 1 maroon, 1 green

ROW 78 — 2 blue and gray mix, 1 green
ROW 79 — 1 blue and gray mix, 1 green, 1 blue
ROWS 80-81 — 1 blue and gray mix, 1 gray, 1 blue

JOY OF LIVING (See illustration)

7 x 10 butted rug which can be enlarged to 9 x 12, 3 ft. center, made by Ruth Henrich, East Longmeadow, Mass.

3 shades of old rose to mahogany for the rose shades, 1, 2, 3, light to dark, 3 shades of aqua to peacock for the blues, 3 shades of gray and much gray tweedy mixture, gold and old gold.

ROWS 1-6 — 1 gray tweed, 1 rose No. 1, 1 light gray tweed
ROWS 7-8 — 1 gray tweed, 2 rose No. 1 (keep rose shades together for diamond)
ROW 9 — 1 gray tweed, 1 rose No. 1, 1 light gray
ROWS 10-12 — 1 gray tweed, 1 rose No. 1, 1 aqua No. 1
ROWS 13-14 — 1 gray tweed, 1 aqua No. 1, 1 aqua No. 2 (keep aquas against aquas when lacing)
ROWS 15-16 — 1 aqua No. 1, 1 aqua No. 2, 1 aqua No. 3
ROWS 17-19 — 1 aqua No. 2, 1 aqua No. 3, 1 gold tweed
ROWS 20-21 — 1 aqua No. 3, 1 light gold, 1 gold tweed
ROW 22 — 1 peacock, 1 light gold, 1 gray (starting peacock diamond)
ROWS 23-24 — 2 peacock blue, 1 gray tweed
ROW 25 — 1 peacock, 1 light gold, 1 gray
ROW 26 — 1 peacock, 2 gray tweed
ROW 27 — 1 peacock, 1 deep gold, 1 gold tweed
ROW 28 — 1 aqua No. 1, 1 aqua No. 2, 1 aqua No. 3
ROW 29 — 2 aqua No. 1, 1 gray
ROW 30 — 1 aqua No. 1, 1 gray, 1 old rose No. 1
ROW 31 — 2 rose No. 2, 1 gray (diagonals in rose)
ROW 32 — 2 rose No. 2, 1 rose No. 3
ROW 33 — 2 rose No. 3, 1 mahogany
ROW 34 — 1 rose No. 3, 2 mahogany
ROWS 35-41 — 1 mahogany, 1 gray, 1 gray tweed
ROWS 42-44 — 2 mahogany, 1 aqua tweed
ROWS 45-48 — 1 mahogany, 1 aqua, 1 charcoal

ROWS 49-50 — 2 dark gray tweed, 1 aqua, 1 rose mahogany

ROWS 51-53 — 1 rose mahogany, 1 aqua, 1 charcoal tweed

ROW 54 — 2 aqua, 1 gold (keep same colors against each other when lacing)

ROWS 55-56 — 1 aqua, 2 gold (keep same colors against each other when lacing)

ROW 57 — 2 aqua, 1 gold (making gold and aqua diamonds)

ROWS 58-60 — 1 aqua No. 1, 1 gray, 1 gray tweed

ROWS 61-62 — 1 aqua No. 1, 1 peacock blue, 1 gray tweed

ROW 63 — 1 aqua No. 2, 1 gray, 1 charcoal

ROWS 64-67 — 1 mahogany, 2 charcoal.

This rug is to be enlarged eventually by introducing the charcoal-gray mixture, with several rows of the deep mahogany shades and the darker grays and gray tweeds.

Mrs. Henrich is a meticulous worker and her braids are about ⅝ inch wide. She does beautiful hooked rugs as well as the braided ones, and I am hoping that some day she will do an outstanding braided border around a hooked center. She is a teacher who has a great future ahead of her. This was the first rug Mrs. Henrich made and won a blue ribbon at Women's International in New York, 1956.

MAINE COMFORT

9 x 12 butted oval—can be made with continuous braid.

Center: 3 ft. long.

ROWS 1-6 — 1 dark blue, 1 blue gray mix., 1 brown and tan mix.

ROW 7 — 1 tan, 1 golden brown, 1 gold and brown mix.

ROW 8 — 1 gold, 1 blue gray mix., 1 lt. rust

ROW 9 — 1 rusty red check, 1 tan mix., 1 blue gray mix.

ROW 10 — 1 rusty red check, 2 dark gray mix.

ROW 11 — 1 rusty red check, 1 dark gray mix., 1 tan mix.

ROW 12 — 1 tan, 1 lt. gray mix., 1 dark gray mix.

ROW 13 — 2 tan mix., 1 dark gray mix.

ROW 14-15 — 1 dark gray mix., 1 tan mix., 1 med. blue

ROW 16-17 — 1 dark gray mix., 1 tan, 1 skipper blue

ROW 18 — 1 dark gray mix., 1 tan, 1 blue mix.

ROWS 19-20 — 2 dark gray mix., 1 blue
ROWS 21-23 — 1 dark gray mix., 2 tan mix.
ROWS 24-27 — 1 dark gray mix., 1 tan mix., 1 blue green
ROWS 28-31 — 1 tan mix., 2 green
ROWS 32-35 — 1 tan, 1 green, 1 brown and gold mix.
ROWS 36-38 — 1 tan, 1 brown, 1 rusty red mix.
ROWS 39-43 — 1 tan mix., 1 rusty red mix.
ROWS 44-49 — 1 tan mix., 1 rusty red, 1 green mix.
ROWS 50-53 — 1 tan mix., 1 rusty red, 1 gold mix.
ROWS 54-56 — 1 tan, 1 gray mix., 1 gold mix.
ROWS 57-58 — 1 tan, 2 gray mix.
ROWS 59-61 — 2 tan mix., 1 gray mix., 1 blue
ROWS 62-65 — 2 gray mix., 1 green tweedy mix.
ROWS 66-68 — 1 dark gray mix., 2 blue gray mixture
ROWS 69-71 — 1 dark gray mix., 1 med. blue, 1 blue and gray mix.
ROWS 72-74 — 1 dark gray mix., 1 med. blue, 1 darker blue
ROWS 75-78 — 1 dark gray mix., 2 dark blue
ROWS 79-81 — 3 dark blue

MEMORY LANE (See illustration)

As these braids were ¾ inch wide, it took 36 rows across to make the 24 in.-wide runner needed. These strips were 30 ft. long, with 1½ in. extra allowed for the turn on each riser. As there was a turn in the stairs which could not be photographed, only the straight part is shown. The turn was accomplished by cutting the braids in pie-shaped wedges and butting the ends together. This is not recommended for the beginner, for the angles must be true and the ends must be butted carefully together at the base of each step, so that no joining shows. Method 7 was used for this.

The last row went all around the lengths and widths, with the enclosed ends butted against this row. Tacks were used on the stairs plus the brass rods, for the runner is heavy.

The color guide for half the runner is given. When making rows for the second side, be sure to put the strips on the safety pin in just the opposite order, so that the colors will lace against each other without any loss of cloth. It is better to do one strip and follow it by its mate for the opposite side.

This runner is pictured in the lovely Cape Cod home of Mr. and Mrs. Thomas Galvin of North Attleboro, Mass. At the foot of the stairs is a 3 x 5 ft. rectangular rug, and at the top in the little square hall is a 48 in. round one. Both rugs pick up the colors of the runner.

Keep same colors against each other when lacing to make the little pattern.

ROW 1 (from the center out) — 1 tan, 2 beige mix.

ROW 2 — 2 tan, 1 beige and tan tweed

ROW 3 — 1 bronze green tweed (green dye over gray tweed), 2 beige and brown mix.

ROW 4 — 1 bronze green tweed, 1 darker green, 1 beige and brown mix.

ROW 5 — 1 darker green, 1 old gold, 1 beige and brown mix.

ROW 6 — 1 medium green, 1 khaki drab, 1 gray and beige tweed

ROW 7 — 1 rust and beige mix., 1 khaki, 1 gray and beige tweed

ROW 8 — 1 rust and beige mix, 1 khaki, 1 tan

ROW 9 — 1 medium tan, 1 dark tan, 1 brown and gold check

ROW 10 — 1 medium tan, 1 dark tan, 1 medium green

ROW 11 — 1 brown, 1 tan, 1 medium green

ROW 12 — 1 dark green, 1 khaki drab, 1 gray and brown tweed

ROW 13 — 1 green, 1 rusty red and gray plaid, 1 tan tweed

ROW 14 — 1 green, 1 brown, 1 tan

ROW 15 — 1 dark green, 1 tan, 1 tan tweed

ROW 16 — 1 dark green, 1 tan, 1 brown tweed

ROW 17 — 1 dark green, 1 brown tweedy mixture, 1 gray and brown tweed

ROW 18 — 2 dark green, 1 brown

MERRY-GO-ROUND

This rug is made up of 3 circles, 26 inches each in diameter. The center one is made up of shaded rounds of rose, pale gold and beige while the 2 outer circles are of shades of aqua, beige and gray going into blue greens. They are bound together with beige and gray mixtures, then there are 9 rows of shaded blue greens and deeper beige mixtures. The circles are tapered off; all other rows are butted in 4 places except the two last rows. These are butted in only one place.

The larger the rug grows, the more shallow becomes the scallop. Eventually, this rug would become an oval in shape, with the difference between the length and the width always the sum of 3 26s or 78 inches. If you desire to make one of these rugs, be sure to figure out before you start, the proper diameter of each of your 3 circles.

Wheels may be made in the same way, using 2 circles instead of 3 as in MERRY-GO-ROUND. One of my pupils made a hall runner with seven 12 inch circles, bordered with 16 rows butted around the whole 7. It was most effective.

NUGGETS OF GOLD

Rectangular rug, 33 x 48 inches.
15 in. center: squared in the braid with sharp squared corners.

ROWS 1-4 — 1 Wedgwood blue, 1 brown tweed flecked with gold, beige and pale gold tweed mixture (keep same colors against each other for diagonal weave)

ROW 5 — 1 Wedgwood blue, 2 pale gold tweedy mix. (keep tweeds against tweeds)

ROW 6 — 1 weak terra cotta, 2 pale gold tweedy mix. (keep tweeds against tweedy mix. of previous row, forming diamonds in tweeds)

ROW 7 — 1 beige and gold tweed, 2 weak terra cotta (keep same colors against each other. This row finishes beige and gold tweed diamond, and is making terra cotta ric-rac)

ROW 8 — 1 beige and gold mix., 1 terra cotta, 1 beige, pale bronze-green and brown mix. (this finishes terra cotta ric-rac)

ROW 9 — 1 beige and gold mix, 1 beige, brown and green mix., 1 tan and beige mix.

ROW 10 — 1 beige, brown and green mix., 1 tan and beige mix., 1 pale bronze-green

ROW 11 — 1 tan and beige mix., 1 green and beige mix., 1 weak bronze

ROW 12 — 1 tan and beige mix., 1 medium bronze, 1 bronze-green mix.

ROW 13 — 1 bronze-green mix., 1 tan and beige mix., 1 brown with gold fleck

ROW 14 — 1 bronze-green mix., 1 brown with gold fleck, 1 gold

ROWS 15-16 — 1 brown with gold fleck, 2 gold (keep golds against golds—forming diamonds)

ROW 17 — 1 brown with gold fleck, 1 gold, 1 medium bronze green

ROW 18 — 1 brown with gold fleck, 1 medium bronze green, 1 bronze-green mix.

ROW 19 — 1 brown and tan mix., 1 bronze green, 1 bronze-green mix.

ROW 20 — 1 medium terra cotta, 1 bronze green, 1 bronze-green mix.

ROW 21 — 2 terra cotta, 1 bronze green (keep terra cottas together)

ROW 22 — 1 terra cotta, 1 pale gold and beige mix., 1 Wedgwood blue (this finishes ric-rac in terra cotta)

ROW 23 — 1 Wedgwood blue, 1 beige and gold mix., 1 brown flecked in gold (keep blues together to start diamonds)

ROWS 24-25 — 2 blues, 1 brown

ROW 26 — 1 blue, 2 brown (arrowheads in brown)

OCTAGON

Continuous braid:

The only trick to making this rug is to make sure that you count off the loops in eight even divisions and keep these sides even throughout the rug.

Start with a circle and make four or five rows. Divide into 8 even sections, putting in T pins to mark off the divisions. Make a square corner at each pin.

If you need to stop and press out to keep it flat, do so, and then go around once without any increases at the points. If at any time the centers of the sides seem too full, make one to three decreases by skipping on the mat itself in the center of the sides. Do it evenly.

Only a few colors are needed in any unusually shaped rug. You can use much or no design as you wish. Only a few rows were put in design "OCTAGON," with one shade of rose, light green, gray tweedy mixture and dark blue used for colors.

ROWS 1-6 — rose, dark blue, gray tweed

ROW 7 — rose, 2 dark blue

ROW 8 — 3 dark blue

ROWS 9-13 — 2 dark blue, gray tweed
ROWS 14-16 — light green, dark blue, gray tweed
ROWS 17-19 — light green, rose, gray tweed
ROWS 20-22 — dark blue, rose, gray tweed
ROW 23 — dark blue, 2 gray tweed
ROW 24 — 2 dark blue, gray tweed
ROW 25 — 3 dark blue

OCTOBER HILLS (See illustration)

9 x 12 ft. rug with continuous braid except for the last three rows which are butted. Pictured in the home of Elynor Crowthers of Franklin, Mass., who made the rug, it blends beautifully with the old pine and maple pieces. The copper lustre pitchers in the hutch (not shown in this picture) pick up and reflect the accent colors. Beige and brown tweedy mixtures make up the background of this rug. The same colors which appear in consecutive rows are laced against each other, to give the whole rug the appearance of a diagonal weave throughout. The rug is a beautiful blend of fall colors.

ROWS 1-10 — 1 beige mixture, 1 tan, 1 brown and beige tweed
ROW 11 — 1 beige mixture, 2 tan
ROWS 12-13 — 1 beige mixture, 1 tan, 1 golden brown
ROWS 14-17 — 1 beige mixture, 1 golden brown, 1 bronze green
ROWS 18-20 — 1 beige mixture, 1 golden brown, 1 gold
ROWS 21-24 — 2 beige mixture, 1 mummy brown
ROWS 25-28 — 1 tan and beige mix., 1 mummy brown, 1 brown and beige tweed
ROWS 29-32 — 1 gold, 1 old gold mix., 1 brown and beige tweed
ROWS 33-36 — 1 tan, 1 rust and tan check, 1 brown and beige tweed
ROWS 37-41 — 1 tan, 1 rust and tan check, 1 hunter green
ROWS 42-45 — 1 tan, 1 gray and brown mix., 1 medium brown
ROWS 46-49 — 2 gray and brown mix., 1 medium brown
ROWS 50-53 — 1 gray and brown mix., 1 spice brown
ROWS 54-58 — 1 beige and brown tweed, 1 old gold, 1 spice brown
ROWS 59-61 — 1 beige and brown tweed, 1 bronze green, 1 tan
ROWS 62-64 — 2 beige and brown tweed, 1 deeper green

ROWS 65-67 — 1 beige and brown tweed, 1 deeper green, 1 brown rust

ROWS 68-72 — 1 tan and brown tweed, 1 olive green, 1 brown rust

ROWS 73-76 — 2 brown and rust tweed, 1 olive green

ROWS 77-79 — 1 brown and rust tweed, 2 olive green

ROWS 80-81 — 2 brown tweed, 1 olive green

OCTOBER SUNSHINE

This is another basic rug which can be enlarged from its present size of 3 x 5 to an 8 x 10 because it has a two ft. center. It can also be used for a color guide for a 9 x 12 by making the center 3 ft. instead of 2 ft. in length.

For a dark room done in pine or maple, the golds and old golds will give a sunshiny effect, and the rusts will warm the pine and maple pieces of furniture. Bronze greens are used to give added warmth while mellowing the golds.

It would be simple to substitute grayed aqua and peacock blues for the greens for a cooler-looking rug, or even blue greens instead of the warm bronze tones. Terra cotta could be used for some of the rusts.

Practically all the material used was beige or gray tiny-checked fleecy light-weight coating, which, when dyed, gives a subtle feeling of close harmony with its adjacent colors.

Three shades of bronze green are used, two with a speck of bright green added for depth of color. There are 3 shades of rust and 1 each of brown rust, tan, medium brown and bronze, 2 shades of gold and of old gold.

Though much design has been used, the colors melt into each other to give a smooth tailored look to the rug instead of having the designs standing out boldly.

Except for the center, the rug is all butted, though the same guide could be used with a continuous braid, for the changes of color are very gradual.

ROWS 1-4 — lt. rust and brown check, gold check, bronze green No. 1

ROW 5 — tan (over gray check), gold check, bronze green No. 1

ROW 6 — medium brown (over gray check), 2 gold mix.

ROW 7 — medium brown, gold mix., tan

ROW 8 — medium brown, bronze, light rust

ROW 9 — bronze, 2 rust

ROW 10 — medium rust, bronze, light rust

ROWS 11-12 — 2 medium rust, brown rust

ROW 13 — 2 medium rust, 2 brown rust

ROWS 14-15 — 2 bronze green No. 1, brown (diamond)

ROW 16 — bronze green No. 2, old gold, brown rust

ROWS 17-18 — pale gold, old gold, bronze green No. 1, (diagonals)

ROW 19 — pale gold, old gold mixture, bronze green No. 1

ROW 20 — light rust, old gold mixture, bronze green No. 2

ROWS 21-22 — lt. rust and brown check, bronze, light rust and gray

ROWS 23-24 — lt. rust and brown check, bronze, medium rust

ROW 25 — lt. rust and brown check, bronze green No. 3, medium rust

ROW 26 — bronze green No. 3, 2 medium rust

ROW 27 — 2 brown rust, medium rust

ROW 28 — 2 brown rust, 1 rusty brown

OLD ARTHRITIS

This 3 x 5 rug gained its name through the fact that it was the first rug I made with round braids. The reason I turned from the small plaited ones was a bout with arthritis. Making the round braid required so little effort that it was far easier on my shoulder and wrist. The name has always appealed to my pupils, particularly to those who have suffered from the same trouble, while the color scheme makes a cheerful-looking rug with its shades of gray and blue, with the accent colors of rose and green giving it added character.

For this rug in which the braids are ¾ in. wide, I used 9 lbs. of materials, with 3½ lbs. gray and gray tweeds; 3 lbs. blues in three shades, light, medium and dark; 1 lb. rose; 1 lb. light tan; ½ lb. greens (ocean green and a green mixture). The rug is a continuous braid except for the last row which is butted.

Center: 2 ft.

ROWS 1-3 — gray tweed, light gray, medium blue
ROWS 4-5 — gray tweed, medium blue, dark blue
ROW 6 — gray tweed, medium blue, rose
ROWS 7-8 — gray tweed, light gray, medium blue, rose
ROW 9 — 2 light gray, medium blue (grays against grays when lacing—arrowheads)
ROWS 10-13 — gray tweed, 2 light gray, medium gray
ROWS 14-15 — gray tweed, 2 light gray, ocean green
ROW 16 — dark tan, 2 light gray, light tan
ROWS 17-18 — medium tan, light tan, green tweed
ROW 19 — gray tweed, light gray, green tweed
ROWS 20-21 — light gray, light tan, rose
ROWS 22-24 — light gray, light tan, 1 light blue
ROW 25 — 1 gray blue, 1 medium blue, 1 light blue
ROWS 26-27 — 1 gray blue, 1 medium blue, 1 dark blue
ROW 28 — 1 medium blue, 2 dark blue (arrowhead when lacing)

This rug has been an inspiration and a comfort to many sufferers of arthritis. It is easy to plan the colors, to find them and to make the rug.

ORIENTALE

Butted oval—40 x 28 inches; 12 inch center.

ROWS 1-3 — 1 medium cherry red, 1 light tan, 1 medium blue, (keep same colors against each other throughout center)
ROWS 4-5 — 1 cherry red, 2 tan (keep same colors against each other to form tan diamonds)
ROW 6 — 1 tan, 1 cherry, 1 pale green (finish diamond in tan)
ROW 7 — 1 cherry, 1 pale green, 1 dark blue (keep greens together)
ROWS 8-9 — 1 cherry, 1 medium aqua blue, 1 dark blue (keep colors against each other to form diagonals)
ROW 10 — 2 soft aqua blue, 1 navy (keep same colors against each other)
ROW 11 — 1 aqua blue, 1 cherry red, 1 dark blue (keeping blues against each other allows this row to finish ric-rac)

ROW 12 — 1 aqua, 1 dark blue, 1 medium beige (keep same colors against each other)

ROW 13 — 1 aqua, blue, 2 beige (keep beige colors against each other, forming ric-rac)

ROW 14 — 1 aqua blue, 1 dark blue, 1 medium beige (this row finishes ric-rac in beige and starts one in blue)

ROW 15 — 1 beige, 2 aqua (using deeper shades now)

ROW 16 — 1 beige, 1 aqua, 1 cherry

ROW 17 — 1 cherry, 2 aqua blue

ROWS 18-19 — 2 cherry, 1 blue (keeping matching colors against each other to form cherry diamonds)

ROW 20 — 1 cherry, 1 blue, 1 dark blue

ROW 21 — 1 blue, 2 dark blue (blues against each other form arrowhead)

PATCHWORK (See illustration)

26 x 38 inches—rectangle with corners squared in the braid.
12 inch center—continuous braid.

ROWS 1-5 — (double rows for center) 1 red, blue and yellow plaid, 1 gray, 1 beige mixture

ROWS 6-7 — 1 blue green, 1 black, 1 gray

ROWS 8-10 — 1 gray, 1 beige, brown and blue mix, 1 black

ROWS 11-12 — 1 gray, 1 beige, 1 gray and blue mix

ROW 13 — 1 beige, 2 gray and blue mix

ROW 14 — 1 beige, 1 red, blue and yellow plaid, 1 gray and blue mix

ROWS 15-16 — 1 red, blue and green plaid, 1 beige and tan mix, 1 gray mix

ROW 17 — 1 gray mix, 1 black, 1 blue green

ROW 18 — 2 black, 1 blue green

PATIENCE

3 x 5 butted rug.

For this rug, you will need to find or to dye terra cotta, Egyptian red, reseda (or grayed blue-greens), and three shades of grayed blues.

I used 2 lbs. of taupe and beige check, 1 lb. of which was dyed terra cotta; 2 lbs. of gray tweedy mixture which I dyed reseda green; 1 lb. of tan; 1½ lbs. brown and blue and beige tiny check; 1 lb. of blues which were softly grayed with the deepest one checked with black; 1 lb. of beige, ½ lb. dyed Egyptian red, and another ½ lb. dyed gold. Terra cotta and Egyptian red are soft brown reds and are especially desirable where there is natural brick, or to give a warm look to an otherwise cool-looking rug. It ties in beautifully with all tans and browns.

Center: 2 ft. long.

ROWS 1-4 — 2 terra cotta, 1 tan (diagonal when lacing)
ROWS 5-6 — 2 terra cotta, 1 tan, reseda green
ROWS 7-9 — 1 tan, 2 reseda green (green diamonds when lacing)
ROWS 10-11 — taupe and beige check, 2 reseda green, gold
ROWS 12-14 — brown and blue mix., 2 reseda green, taupe and tan check
ROW 15 — brown and blue mix., reseda green, Egyptian red
ROWS 16-18 — 1 green, 2 Egyptian red (diamonds)
ROWS 19-20 — 1 green, taupe and beige check, 2 Egyptian red
ROW 22 — 1 tan, taupe and beige check, 1 blue No. 1
ROWS 22-23 — blue No. 2, taupe and beige check, 1 blue No. 1
ROWS 24-25 — 2 blue No. 2, 1 gray green
ROW 26 — blue No. 3, 1 gray green, blue No. 2
ROW 27 — 2 blue No. 3, 1 gray green

POT O' GOLD

8 x 10 butted oval, may be made with continuous braid. Pictured in the home of Mrs. Carl A. Carlson, Westboro, Mass.—3 shades turquoise blue. Center is 2 ft. long.

Rows 1-8 — Keep same colors against each other when lacing.

ROW 8 — 1 blue No. 2 shade, 1 blue check, 1 gold and dark brown tweed
ROW 9 — 2 blue No. 2 shade, 1 blue check, forming blue ric-rac
ROW 10 — 1 blue No. 2 shade, 1 blue check, 1 terra cotta and beige tweed

ROWS 11-12 — 1 blue check, 1 light bronze-green tweed mixture, 1 terra cotta mix.

ROW 13 — 2 bronze-green mix., 1 terra cotta mix., (ric-rac in green)

ROW 14 — 1 bronze-green mix., 2 terra cotta mix., (terra cottas together when lacing)

ROW 15 — 1 bronze-green mix., 1 terra cotta mix., 1 pale terra cotta

ROWS 16-17 — 2 bronze-green mix., 1 pale terra cotta (green diamonds)

ROW 18 — 1 bronze-green mix., 1 terra cotta No. 2 shade, 1 pale gold

ROWS 19-20 — 1 gold, 1 terra cotta No. 2, 1 medium brown

ROWS 21-23 — 1 old gold, 2 med. brown, (double brown diamonds)

ROWS 24-25 — 1 old gold, 1 med. brown, 1 blue No. 1 shade

ROW 26 — 1 blue and tan tweed, 1 blue No. 1 shade, 1 blue No. 2 shade

ROW 27 — 1 blue and brown tweed, 1 blue No. 1 shade, 1 blue No. 2 shade

ROWS 28-29 — 1 blue and brown tweed, 1 blue No. 2 shade, 1 blue No. 3 shade

ROW 30 — 1 blue and brown tweed, 1 tan and beige tweed, 1 blue No. 3 shade

ROW 31 — 2 blue and brown tweed, 1 tan

ROW 32 — 1 blue and brown tweed, 1 tan, 1 blue and beige tweed

ROW 33 — 1 blue and beige tweed, 1 tan, 1 blue, brown and beige check

ROW 34 — 1 blue and beige tweed, 1 gold and blue mix., 1 blue and brown check

ROWS 35-36 — 1 golden brown mix., 1 gold and blue mix., 1 blue and beige tweed

ROWS 37-39 — 1 golden brown mix., 1 tan, 1 bronze green

ROWS 40-41 — 1 golden brown mix., 2 bronze-green (green diamonds)

ROW 42 — 1 golden brown mix., 1 bronze-green

ROW 43 — 1 golden brown mix., 1 bronze-green 2nd shade, 1 terra cotta

ROWS 44-45 — 2 bronze-green 2nd shade, 1 terra cotta

ROW 46 — 1 bronze-green 2nd shade, 1 old gold, 1 terra cotta

ROWS 47-48 — 1 old gold, 2 brown, (brown diamonds)

ROWS 49-50 — 1 old gold, 1 brown, 1 blue No. 1 shade

ROW 51 — 1 blue No. 1 shade, 2 blue No. 2 shade

ROW 52 — 1 blue No. 2 shade, 2 blue No. 3 shade

ROWS 53-55 — 1 blue No. 2 shade, 1 blue No. 3 shade, 1 gold and black tweed mix.

ROW 56 — 1 gold and black tweed mix., 2 blue No. 3 shade

ROW 57 — 2 blue No. 3 shade, 1 blue and beige mix.

ROWS 58-59 — 1 bronze-green and brown mix., 1 blue and beige mix., 1 terra cotta

ROW 60 — 1 bronze-green and brown mix., 1 bronze-green, 1 terra cotta

ROW 61 — 2 bronze-green, 1 terra cotta, (forming green ric-rac)

ROW 62 — 1 bronze-green, 1 terra cotta, 1 pale gold

ROW 63 — 1 brown, 1 terra cotta, 1 deeper gold

ROWS 64-66 — 1 brown, 2 old gold, (forming gold diamonds)

ROWS 67-68 — 2 brown, 1 old gold

ROW 69 — 1 brown, 1 tan, 1 blue No. 2 shade

ROW 70 — 1 gold and brown mix., 1 blue No. 2 shade, 1 blue No. 3 shade

ROWS 71-72 — 1 gold and brown mix., 2 blue No. 3 shade

RHAPSODY IN BLUE

Many requests are always coming in for a guide in blues and browns. This particular one has been worked out in a 9 ft. round rug with a continuous braid except for the last two rows. I am giving it for a 9 x 12 size, which means that the center will be 3 ft. long, but the directions are the same for a 9 ft. round rug. If you want to make it 8 x 10, make a 2 ft. center and omit nine rows, if you braid a ¾ in.-wide braid.

Colors used: beige and brown mix., and beige and blue tweed for background; tan, golden brown, medium brown, spice brown, brown, aqualon blue, turquoise blue (3 shades), peacock

Center: 3 ft. long. Keep same colors against each other when lacing to form patterns.

ROWS 1-10 — 1 beige, 2 beige and brown mix.

ROWS 11-13 — 2 beige, 1 beige and brown mix.

ROWS 14-16 — 2 beige, 1 beige and brown mix., 1 tan

ROWS 17-19 — 1 beige, 1 turquoise 1st shade, 1 tan

ROWS 20-22 — beige and brown mix., 1 turquoise No. 1, 1 turquoise 2nd shade

ROWS 23-24 — beige and brown mix., 2 turquoise 2nd shade

ROW 25 — 3 turquoise 2nd shade

ROWS 26-27 — 2 turquoise 2nd shade, 1 beige and brown mix.

ROWS 28-29 — 1 turquoise 2nd shade, 1 beige and brown mix., 1 beige and blue tweed

ROWS 30-33 — 1 golden brown, 1 beige and brown mix., 1 beige and blue tweed

ROWS 34-35 — 2 golden brown, 1 beige and brown mix.

ROWS 36-38 — 1 golden brown, beige and brown mix., 1 tan and brown tweed

ROWS 39-40 — 1 golden brown, 1 medium brown, 1 tan and brown tweed

ROWS 41-43 — 1 golden brown, 2 medium brown

ROW 44 — 3 medium brown

ROWS 45-46 — 2 medium brown, 1 tan and brown tweed

ROWS 47-49 — 1 golden brown, 1 aqualon blue, 1 tan and brown tweed

ROWS 50-51 — 1 turquoise No. 1 shade, 1 aqualon blue, 1 tan and brown tweed

ROWS 52-53 — 1 turquoise No. 2 shade, 1 beige and blue tweed, 1 tan tweed

ROWS 54-56 — 2 turquoise No. 2 shade, 1 tan tweed

ROWS 57-58 — 1 turquoise No. 2 shade, 1 turquoise No. 3 shade, 1 tan tweed

ROW 59 — 1 turquoise No. 2 shade, 2 turquoise No. 3 shade

ROWS 60-61 — 2 turquoise No. 3 shade, 1 tan tweed

ROWS 62-64 — 1 beige and blue tweed, 1 turquoise No. 3 shade, 1 tan tweed

ROWS 65-66 — 1 beige and brown tweed, 1 tan tweed, 1 beige and blue tweed

ROW 67 — 1 golden brown, 1 tan tweed, 1 beige and blue tweed

ROWS 68-69 — 1 golden brown, 1 tan tweed, 1 medium brown

ROW 70 — 1 golden brown, 2 medium brown

ROWS 71-72 — 3 medium brown

ROWS 73-74 — 2 medium brown, 1 tan tweed

ROW 75 — 1 medium brown, 1 tan tweed, 1 turquoise No. 3 shade

ROWS 76-77 — 1 medium brown, 1 spice brown, 1 peacock
ROWS 78-79 — 2 spice brown, 1 peacock
ROW 80 — 1 brown, 2 spice brown
ROW 81 — 2 brown, 1 spice brown

If you prefer the soft grayed blues to the green blues, use them in three shades with perhaps skipper blue and navy. The latter will provide a nice accent.

ROULETTE

Round butted rug, 42 in. in diameter, no increases except where noted.

Three colors only—red, black, gray and black mixture.

6 inch center (4 rows): Increase plenty on last two rows, none on the next two. Taper off.

ROW 5 — 1 black, 2 grays (keep grays against gray, black against black)

ROW 6 — 2 black, 1 gray (keep same colors against each other. You have now finished gray ric-rac and black arrowhead)

ROW 7 — 1 red, 1 black, 1 gray (increase plenty, none on next two rows)

ROW 8 — 2 red, 1 gray (same colors against each other)

ROWS 9-10 — first row finishes red ric-rac (increase plenty on 10th row)

ROW 11 — 2 gray, 1 black (same colors against each other)

ROW 12 — 2 black, 1 gray (this row finishes gray ric-rac and black arrowhead)

ROW 13 — 3 black (increase plenty)

ROW 14 — 2 black, 1 gray (increase plenty)

ROW 15 — 1 black, 2 gray (same colors matching those of previous row)

ROWS 16-18 — 1 black, 1 red, 1 gray (increase plenty if needed. If not needed keep same colors together to form diagonals)

ROW 19 — 2 red, 1 gray (forming red ric-rac)

ROWS 20-23 — 1 red, 2 gray (gray diagonals, lost occasionally if you need to increase to keep the rug flat)

ROWS 24-26 — 1 red, 1 black, 1 gray mix (keeping same colors to-gether as much as possible)

ROWS 27-28 — 1 black, 2 gray mixtures (forming gray diamonds)

ROW 29 — 2 black, 1 gray mix (finish gray diamonds, making black arrowheads)

ROW 30 — 3 black, enough increases to keep rug flat

SHINING WATERS

Rectangle, 28 x 50, beautiful rug done for a modern home, in turquoise and white, with silver lurex thread woven in the woolen materials used. 3½ yards of white are used, with 3¼ yards of turquoise dyed over a pale aqua blue with a dye solution of 4 teaspoonfuls to each batch of strips. This means that 1 teaspoonful of dry turquoise dye was first dissolved in 1 cup of hot water, and this solution is used for the dyeing.

The silver threads are not affected by the dye bath, and give a shimmering appearance to the whole rug.

Continuous braid with the center 22 in. long.

ROWS 1-6 — 3 white

ROWS 7-8 — 2 white, 1 turquoise. By keeping turquoise away from each other in adjacent rows, you will have turquoise "jewels" and will also form white rosettes or "flowers" of white.

ROW 9 — 2 turquoise, 1 white. Turquoise arrowheads when lacing

ROW 10 — 3 turquoise

ROWS 11-13 — 2 turquoise, 1 white. Whites against whites when lacing.

ROW 14 — 3 turquoise

ROW 15 — 2 turquoise, 1 white

ROWS 16-19 — 1 turquoise, 1 white. Jewels in turquoise and white flowers will be formed by keeping opposite colors against each other when lacing.

SILVER GLINTS

Rectangle, 26 x 37, made with sharp square corners turned in the braid, by Virginia Ingram, Stamford, Conn. Made with a continuous braid of poodle cloth, shot with metallic silver threads. 12 inch center.

Center Rows 1-4—1 pale rust, 1 beige, 1 light blue.

ROW 5 — 1 beige, 2 lt. blue, (blues against blues in preceding row)
ROW 6 — 1 beige, 1 lt. blue, 1 medium rust, (finish blue ric-rac)
ROW 7 — 1 beige, 2 med. rust, (forming rust ric-rac)
ROW 8 — 1 beige, 1 med. rust, 1 light blue
ROWS 9-10 — 1 light blue, 1 med. blue, 1 rust
ROWS 11-12 — 2 blue, 1 rust, (blues against blues in preceding rows to form diagonals)
ROW 13 — 1 blue, 1 rust, 1 med. brown
ROW 14 — 1 blue, 1 rust, 1 dark blue
ROW 15 — 2 dark blue, 1 rust (keep blues against each other when lacing, for diamonds)
ROW 16 — 2 dark blue, 1 med. brown, (start brown ric-rac)
ROW 17 — 1 dark blue, 2 med. brown
ROW 18 — 1 med. rust, 1 med. brown, 1 med. blue (finish ric-rac)
ROW 19 — 1 med. rust, 1 brown rust, 1 med. blue
ROW 20 — 1 med. rust, 1 brown rust, 1 darker blue

This is an unusually pretty rug, with a gleam of silver over the entire surface. It lifts the rug quite out of the commonplace and puts it into the luxury class.

STARLIGHT (See illustration)

Star within a star—5 points—each row butted except the center circle. If carried out far enough the star will again become a circle.

Center circle—6 complete rounds for a 9 in. diameter—3 beige mix.

ROW 7 — 1 light aqua, 2 light beige tweed mixture
ROW 8 — 1 pale yellow, 1 beige mix, 1 light aqua mix. This goes out in 5 inch long points at 5 even spaces to form points of star
ROWS 9-10 — 1 pale yellow, 1 aqua mix, 1 light blue gray mix
ROWS 11-12 — 1 pale yellow, 1 aqua mix, 1 light beige mix
ROWS 13-15 — 1 pale yellow, 1 gray mix, 1 beige mix
ROWS 16-18 — 1 light grayblue, 1 beige, 1 gray

ROW 19 — 1 light grayblue, 1 beige, 1 gray
ROWS 20-21 — 1 light grayblue, 1 beige, 1 pale yellow
ROW 22 — 2 light blue, 1 medium blue
ROWS 23-27 — 1 grayblue, 2 medium blue
ROWS 28-29 — 1 light blue, 2 medium blue

TRANQUILLITY

Rectangle 6 ft. 2 in. x 8 ft. 2 in.
Center: 2 ft. long—continuous braid.

ROWS 1-6 — 1 old rose check, 1 mauve, 1 taupe
ROWS 7-8 — 2 old rose check, 1 mauve
ROW 9 — 1 old rose check, 1 mauve, 1 weak mahogany dyed over gray
ROWS 10-11 — 1 old rose check, 1 mahogany, 1 golden brown
ROWS 12-13 — 1 mahogany, 1 golden brown, 1 weak reseda green
ROW 14 — 1 gray green, 2 golden brown (now forming brown diagonals)
ROW 15 — 1 golden brown, 1 taupe, 1 brownish gray
ROW 16 — 1 soft gray blue, 1 taupe, 1 golden brown
ROWS 17-18 — 1 soft gray blue, 1 taupe, 1 gray
ROWS 19-21 — 1 soft gray blue, 1 gray, 1 gray and blue check
ROW 22 — 1 gray, 2 gray and blue check
ROW 23 — 1 gray, 1 gray and blue check, 1 taupe
ROWS 24-26 — 1 gray, 2 taupe
ROWS 27-29 — 2 taupe, 1 gray green
ROW 30 — 1 taupe, 1 gray green, 1 golden brown and beige check
ROWS 31-32 — 1 tan, 1 gray green, 1 golden brown and beige check
ROW 33 — 1 gray green, 1 old rose check, 1 golden brown and beige check
ROW 34 — 1 light mahogany, 1 old rose check, 1 golden brown and beige check
ROWS 35-37 — 1 light mahogany, 1 old rose check, 1 mulberry
ROWS 38-40 — 1 spice brown, 1 rose check, 1 mulberry (colors against the same colors in previous rows—mulberry diagonals)
ROW 41 — 2 mulberry, 1 rose check
ROW 42 — 1 mulberry, 1 rose check, 1 dark beige

ROW 43 — 1 rose check, 1 brown and beige check, 1 gray blue mix.
ROWS 44-46 — 1 gray blue mix., 1 brown and beige check, 1 taupe
ROWS 47-49 — 1 taupe, 1 gray blue check, 1 spice brown
ROWS 50-52 — 1 taupe, 1 light tan, 1 brown
ROWS 53-54 — 1 taupe, 1 light tan, 1 olive green
ROW 55 — 1 light tan, 2 olive green
ROWS 56-57 — 1 light tan, 1 olive green, 1 brown
ROW 58 — 1 light tan, 2 brown (arrowhead in brown)

TWINKLETOES

For my little granddaughter Susan Ingram's room which is decorated in pink and green with a bed covered with her great-great-grandmother's old coverlet worked painstakingly in pinks and greens and quilted on a creamy white background, I made "TWINKLETOES," a colorful butted 3 x 5 rug with a shaded blue center which blends gradually into the pink and rose shades in the little apple blossoms on the wall paper, the delicate pink of the two painted walls, and the pink dust-ruffle of the old hand-carved four-poster on which so many of her forebears have slept.

The rose blends out into pale leaf greens, then the darker tones into beige, tan and the brown woodsy tones.

For this rug, you will need to dye three shades of pink to rose, three shades of the lighter blues into the medium and dark tones, three shades of green, and three shades of brown.

Center: 2 ft. long.

ROWS 1-4 — 2 blue No. 1 shade, 1 blue No. 2
ROW 5 — 1 blue No. 1 shade, 2 blue No. 2 shade
ROW 6 — 2 third shade blue, 1 first shade pink
ROW 7 — 1 third shade blue, 2 first shade pink
ROW 8 — 2 first shade pink, 1 second shade pink
ROWS 9-10 — 2 pink No. 2, 1 rose pink No. 3
ROW 11 — 2 rose No. 3, 1 pale green
ROWS 12-13 — 1 rose No. 3, 2 pale green
ROWS 14-15 — 2 green shade No. 1, 1 green shade No. 2
ROWS 16-18 — 2 green No. 2, 1 green No. 3
ROW 19 — 2 green No. 3, 1 beige

ROW 20 — 2 beige, 1 tan
ROWS 21-22 — 1 beige, 1 tan, 1 golden brown
ROWS 23-24 — 1 tan, 2 golden brown
ROWS 25-26 — 1 golden brown, 1 medium brown, 1 brown
ROW 27 — 1 medium brown, 2 brown

VICTORIAN ELEGANCE (See illustration)

This 30 inch center is hooked—a trio of roses in yellow gold, gray-white and rose-red surrounded by leaves and buds on a marbleized background of beiges, tans and grays. This is edged by "flames" of all the colors used in the center. The first row of braid is sewn to the tape but all the other rows are laced and each one is, of course, butted. They shade from the lightest shades of gray and beige out to the gold, green and rose shades into the darkest shades of green and brown.

Good proportion for a braided edge is from ⅛ to ½ of the width of the hooked center. Use few colors on the edge; the beauty of many hooked centers is enhanced by monochromatic borders, shading from light to dark.

WELCOME MAT (See illustration)

This rug is included through the courtesy of the *American Home Magazine* which has done much to raise standards of braiding throughout the country. To obtain specific directions for this unusual rug, send to *American Home Magazine,* Pattern Dept., 300 Park Ave., New York, N.Y.

Cost of pattern is listed below with number of pattern:

Welcome mat no. 1598—30¢

WINTER CARNIVAL

This square-cornered 7 x 9 rug was made by Doris Hanan in the Lynn, Mass., Evening School of Practical Arts. The teacher was Mrs. Arlene Fisher, well-known teacher on the North Shore whose spring exhibitions always are outstanding, with several room-sized rugs attracting hundreds of visitors. These large rugs are made with continuous small braids, beautifully blended with rich harmonizing colors, and the last few rows are always butted.

For "WINTER CARNIVAL," light and medium gray and black are used with three shades of red, two shades of green, and two shades of old gold.

The color guide for this rug could be enlarged to any size, with wider bands or through repetition, but with the 2 ft. center lengthened to 3 ft. for a 6 x 9 or 9 x 12. This one has a 2 ft. center.

ROWS 1-8 — old gold, bright red, light gray
ROWS 9-12 — bright red, 2 light gray
ROWS 13-16 — bright red, light gray, medium gray
ROWS 17-18 — bright red, medium gray, black
ROW 19 — 2 red, black
ROWS 20-21 — red, medium gray, black
ROWS 22-23 — old gold shade 2, medium gray, black
ROWS 24-26 — old gold, light gray, medium gray
ROWS 27-28 — 2 light gray, medium gray
ROWS 29-31 — light gray, 2 medium gray
ROW 32 — light gray, medium gray, black
ROWS 33-34 — 2 medium gray, black
ROWS 35-38 — green, 2 medium gray, black
ROWS 39-40 — green, 2 medium gray
ROWS 41-42 — green, gold, medium gray
ROWS 43-44 — gold, lt. gray, black
ROWS 45-47 — medium gray, gold, black
ROW 48 — medium gray, green, black
ROW 49 — 2 medium gray, green
ROW 50 — 3 medium gray
ROWS 51-52 — 2 medium gray, maroon
ROWS 53-54 — medium gray, 2 maroon
ROWS 55-56 — 2 medium gray, maroon
ROW 57 — 3 medium gray

SOURCES OF MATERIALS
AND SUPPLIES

Berry Paper Stock Co., Dean St., Taunton, Mass., (everything for braiders)
Quality Coat Co., Elm and Orange Sts., New Haven, Conn.
Franklin Mill Store, Union St., Franklin, Mass.
Natick Mill Outlet, Natick, Mass.
Heller and Michaelson, Charles St., Providence, R.I.
Cushing Perfection Dye Co., Dover-Foxcroft, Maine
Heather Shop, Lebanon, N.H.
Carlbert Rug Supplies, Fore St., Portland, Me.
Hylan's, Pleasant St., Arlington, Mass.
May Woolens, Inc., 311 West 8th St., Kansas City, Mo.
Mill Ends, Inc., 204 West 8th St., Kansas City, Mo.
Colonial Remnant Shoppe, Manchester, Conn.

There are many remnant shops and mill end stores throughout the country which have excellent woolens for rug braiding. There are many mills also where one may buy remnants, but they do not cater to mail order business. Several places advertise regularly, and the braiders must be alert to finding supplies as near their homes as possible. Here in New England we have many fine sources and are more fortunate than those in the West. With the trend toward rug braiding, however, I am constantly hearing of more and more remnant shops for rug supplies being opened up in the middle and far western states. Braid-aids, woolens and lacing cord, and lacers of various kinds may be purchased in the needlecraft department of all large stores.

INDEX